FREMDENBLATT
LISTE DES ÉTRANGERS
LIST OF VISITORS
BADEN
SCHWEIZ · SUISSE
THERMAL- KURORT
BAINS SULFUREUX
ART. ANSTALT A. TRÜB & Co. AARAU.

TAKING *the* WATERS

Spirit
Art
Sensuality

Alev Lytle Croutier

Abbeville Press • Publishers
New York • London • Paris

Jacket front: Sir Lawrence Alma-Tadema, The Baths of Caracalla. *See p. 83.*

Jacket back: Roman Irish bath at Friedrichsbad, Baden-Baden, Germany.

Half-title page: Galileo Chini, detail of a fresco (1922) on the wall of the grand staircase of the Berzieri Baths, Salsomaggiore, Italy.

Frontispiece: Poster, Baden, Switzerland.

Copyright page: Henri Edmond Cross, L'Histoire de l'eau, *1894, bas-relief, 90½ × 32⅜ × 19⅝ in. (230 × 82 × 50 cm). Musée d'Orsay, Paris.*

Dedication page: John Atkinson Grimshaw, Endymion on Mount Latmus, *1879+, oil on canvas, 32 × 47 in. (81.28 × 119.38 cm). Private collection.*

pp. 10–11, 74–75, and 184–85: Detail of the tile work at the Berzieri Baths, Salsomaggiore, Italy.

EDITOR: Jacqueline Decter
DESIGNER: Patricia Fabricant
PICTURE RESEARCHERS: Adrienne Aurichio,
    Deborah Abramson
COPY CHIEF: Robin James
COPY EDITOR: Clifford Browder
PRODUCTION SUPERVISOR: Hope Koturo

First edition

Library of Congress Cataloging-in-Publication
    Data
Croutier, Alev Lytle, 1944–
    Taking the waters: spirit, art, sensuality /
    Alev Lytle Croutier.
        p.   cm.
    Includes bibliographical references and
        index.
    ISBN 1-55859-219-9
    1. Bathing customs.   2. Baths.
    3. Health resorts.   4. Water — Folklore.
    5. Water in art.   I. Title.
GT2845.C76   1992
391'.64 — dc20   92-15691
                                                   CIP

To Robert

Love's fire heats water, water cools not love.

WILLIAM SHAKESPEARE, "Sonnet 154"

Contents

Water is H$_2$O
Hydrogen two parts
Oxygen one
But there is also a third thing
That makes it water.
And nobody knows what that is.
D. H. LAWRENCE

Preface

I am writing this book sitting in a well house, a tank containing an enormous amount of water above my head, constantly pumping. Sometimes I fantasize that a water spirit is overseeing me writing a book about itself. Other times I fear that the tank might burst from pressure and I could perish in a deluge.

Out of my window I see a panorama of a vast ocean, waves crashing, whales migrating, fishing boats docked around the reef, and in the distance, meticulously painted ocean liners crossing the horizon. I'm thinking of the book I'm writing about water. I'm thinking of the ways that water has touched me in my own life and continues to without my even knowing it.

Water is the most valuable element in our lives. It is a dancer of many forms. It makes sounds of many pitches, passionate, soothing, and ethereal. Water's hypnotic innocence hides nothing and yet it is still a mystery, full of endless associations, sacred and profane, creative and destructive.

Curiously, I was born under the sign of Aquarius—the Water Bearer— in a house facing the sea, and in my life now I am living in a house facing another sea. Wherever I go, I look for sources of water—the ocean, hot springs, or great baths. But I'm also terrified of water, having almost drowned twice and survived a major flood. The last San Francisco earthquake caught me, of all places, sitting in a bathtub full of water.

Everyone has their water stories and tales; without much provocation, they seem to pour out. Many of mine took place on the Aegean coast of Turkey when I was a child. I'd often see, out of my grandparents' window, a sad donkey pacing round and round, and the waterwheel turning. Or watch the nomads riding their camels—magnificent animals with water storage cells in their stomachs that render them invaluable for desert crossing. Sometimes I'd catch a glimpse of my grandmother talking to the well or throwing coins into it when no one seemed to be watching. Sometimes I did the same.

We lived through endless seasons of drought when not a drop of water fell, and what the reservoirs contained was rationed out infrequently. As

Benjamin Franklin's *Poor Richard's Almanac* observes: "When the well's dry, we know the worth of water." Imagine turning on your faucet and nothing comes out but a mocking hiss. Imagine not being able to bathe, flush the toilet, or wash soiled diapers for days, sometimes weeks! But the drought motivated us to take clay jugs and buckets and draw water from a central fountain. Soon this became a special watering place where women gathered and enjoyed social encounters and shared gossip. Around the corner, men found their pleasure in teahouses, smoking waterpipes.

I recall many times when my father dragged us to a country spa where we endured sulfurous humidity and were forced to drink horrible-tasting waters: because they were supposed to make us healthier and live longer, it was all right to suffer.

My fascination with the philosophy of bathing began in 1989, when *Art & Antiques* magazine asked me to write an article on baths in art. I recalled that the house in which I was born had a *hamam,* or communal bathhouse. It was fun and mysterious. When, a few years later, my family moved into a modern apartment that boasted a shower and privacy, I missed those rituals. Fortunately, I returned to the world of hamams when I attended a girls' boarding school in Istanbul. Every Saturday morning, trailing *bornozes* and clacking *pattens*, we slithered into a hamam with brilliant tile walls and marble sinks. Then a twelve-year-old, I was entering the most exclusive society of young voluptuaries, in which the older girls flaunted their bodies before us as a form of territorial gesture. Bathing, I discovered, was an art—of silent abandon and sensuality.

Moments of intimacy with water are endless. In my research I focused on the metaphysical, aesthetic, and rejuvenative aspects of the liquid element. I discovered how water has been a spiritual force in people's lives everywhere—and still is—and how wells, springs, and streams were worshiped because of their ability to heal. And how over the centuries these same sacred waters have evolved into popular baths and spas. I saw the manner in which this evolution mirrors and reflects the changing morals and attitudes of our society.

There are literally thousands of watering places in the world, ranging from secluded hot springs on the tops of mountains to the splendid spas of nineteenth-century European aristocracy. I made my selection among those that, rich in history, still manage to maintain the integrity of their waters and the spirit of the place. The spas I visited shared with me not only the mythology of their waters but also the world surrounding them, and became part of my personal mythology. Usually only a privileged few have access to these places, but through the generosity of many people I was also able to indulge in taking the waters and rejoice in how water has always influenced art, architecture, music, and cinema.

Water has its own language. I believe that by observing the ways that people have danced with it throughout history, we can gain a deeper awareness of this most precious element. A responsible appreciation of water is fundamental to our ecological, environmental, and spiritual values.

A.L.C.

THE
SPIRIT
OF WATER

Myths

The Noblest Element

Water has always been celebrated as a source of energy—physical and metaphysical. Natural philosophers recognized it as the source of living formative processes that they called "the sensitive chaos." Goethe regarded it as the universal element; Pindar referred to it as "the noblest element." Leonardo da Vinci postulated a method of exploring water from every angle, from the smallest drop to the largest rivers. For him it was full of paradox:

> *Water is sometimes sharp and sometimes strong, sometimes acid and sometimes bitter, sometimes sweet and sometimes thick or thin, sometimes it is seen bringing hurt or pestilence, sometimes health-giving, sometimes poisonous. It suffers change into as many natures as are the different places through which it passes. And as the mirror changes with the color of its object, so it alters with the nature of the place, becoming: noisome, laxative, astringent, sulfurous, salty, incarnadined, mournful, raging, angry, red, yellow, green, black, blue, greasy, fat or slim. Sometimes it starts a conflagration, sometimes it extinguishes one; is warm and is cold, carries away or sets down, hollows out or builds up, tears down or establishes, fills or empties, raises itself or burrows down, speeds or is still; is the cause at times of life or death, or increase or*

William Bouguereau, La Naissance de Vénus, 1879, oil on canvas, 118 x 85¾ in. (300 x 218 cm). Musée d'Orsay, Paris

privation, nourishes at times and at others does the contrary; at times has a tang, at times is without savor, sometimes submerging the valleys with great floods. In time and with water, everything changes.

The creative and destructive elements of water elevated it to a metaphysical realm. As the medieval German poet Wolfram von Eschenbach wrote in *Parcival:* "From water, trees derive their sap. Water fructifies all created things, which man calls creatures. From water man has sight. Water gives many souls such radiance that angels cannot be more bright."

Myths of Creation

Why did the Persians hold the sea holy? Why did the Greeks give it a separate deity, and own brother of Jove? Surely all this is not without meaning.
HERMAN MELVILLE, *Moby Dick*

Among ancient civilizations, water was sanctified as the source of life, the seminal fluid, the juice of the earth's womb. It formed a common thread in their creation myths. The act of creation was perceived by the primitives as the catharsis of a dance that the great deities performed. These deities were the elements, inseparable and interdependent systems orchestrating the cycles of nature, the seasons, and the sustenance of all beings. Water could not exist without earth, fire, or air. There was no fragmentation yet.

Liquid, colorless, and transparent, water is a cosmic mirror, reflecting everything back to the source—creatures, mountains, clouds. The image of water as the mirror of the universe persisted all the way into the world religions. "God created the heavens and the earth. The earth was without form and void, and darkness was upon the face of the deep; and the Spirit of God was moving over the face of the waters," reads the Book of Genesis.

Since almost every civilization assumed that life began in the sea, the word for "sea" is feminine in many languages and is everywhere connected with emerging life. In Sumerian, for example, *mar* meant "womb" as well as "sea." The Sumerians believed that in the beginning there was only the calm sea under the vast emptiness of the sky, waiting to be touched by the storm god Huracan. When she was, the earth came out of the *mar.*

Marine biologist Lyall Watson makes a similar analogy in *The Water Planet* (1988): "With moods that mirror ours, ranging from ripples of interest and awareness, to the savage seas of rage and fury. And through all these manifestations, it carries a maternal voice and reminders of the womb."

In a Japanese creation myth a giant carp awoke from its slumber under the sea. It thrashed around so violently that it caused an enormous tidal wave (*tsunami*), out of which the "earth," in the form of the Japanese islands, arose.

While the Indian god Vishnu was reclining on the cosmic serpent, which was floating on the cosmic waters, he willed the earth into existence.

On the plains of North America where Apache, Pima, and Blackfoot lived, all was still until Old Man arrived, floating on his raft and willing the earth into existence out of the water. Other North American Indian tribes described how the creator sent an animal down to the bottom of the sea to bring up mud, out of which he made the earth. They also mythologized the Earth Diver, who brought up the land from the primal water. Yet they were unaware that, beyond the oceans, people unknown to them shared similar myths describing the act of creation. The Sumerian and Akkadian Apsu, for instance, was the primordial chaos, the sweet-water ocean underlying the earth, which was united with the goddess Tiamat at the beginning of time.

Ancient Water Deities

Every early civilization deified the elements. Some water deities were good, others evil, but all were powerful, usually omnipotent, and always capable of controlling the destinies of human beings. People everywhere feared, revered, or worshiped them. Although these gods differed in name and form from culture to culture, all shared the fundamental creative and destructive substance of water.

In the Fertile Crescent, the Assyro-Babylonian people worshiped water as the primordial element that came from Apsu, an abyss surrounding the earth; they personified it as Enki or Ea—the creator of life-giving springs, lakes, and streams. (Ea is also credited with befriending Noah and advising him to build an ark in order to avoid the great deluge.) Canopus in Egypt, Apah in India, and Aleyin in Phoenecia were all versions of gods who emerged from Apsu.

The goddess Anahita of Chaldea and Persia, known as the Immaculate One, personified the earth's seminal fluid flowing from the stars. An archetype of Artemis, she was also the goddess of the fertilizing waters whose humid influences, pouring down from the heavens, gave fecundity to the earth.

In Japanese mythology the word *umi* (ocean) is homophonous with the word meaning "to give birth," and many of the ancient Japanese deities were conceived through contact with the sea. The sea god, later called the dragon king, lived beneath the waves with his daughters and female attendants, much like the Olympian water deities.

Many deities, demiurges, and heroes, whose parents are often nameless, absent, or ambiguous, emerged from water. For example, Sargon, the founder of Babylon, whose past is unknown, was rescued from the reeds

The Egyptian goddess Nut symbolized the flowing unity of celestial primordial waters. Later on she reappeared in Greek myth as the Cretan princess Ariadne and the goddess Aphrodite.

by the water carrier Akki. Karna, a hero of the Indian epic *The Mahabharata,* was discovered floating on the Ganges. Aphrodite rose out of a seashell from sea foam. While bathing in the Nile, the pharaoh's daughter discovered Moses—whose name means "water drawer"—floating in a basket. All these survivors came into their own power allied with the forces of water.

Malevolent Waters

The Chinese feared the sea. Like the Balinese, they perceived an angry sea populated by strange, menacing spirits that scared away intruders. Sedna, the Eskimo goddess of sea animals and master of whales, possessed malevolent attributes. The Zulus, because they believed that a beast inhabited the waters, resisted looking into sources of water lest the beast steal their souls. Losing one's soul implied losing one's life, because the body could not sustain itself without the nourishment of the soul.

The natives of the Andaman Islands in the Bay of Bengal, convinced that their reflection was actually their soul, avoided looking in the water. Similarly in ancient Greece and India, if people dreamed of seeing their reflections in the water, it was an omen that they would soon die. They also feared that water spirits would drag the soul under water, leaving a person soulless for the journey ahead.

All this excites our suspicion that the Narcissus legend, in which a beautiful youth falls in love with his own reflection in the water—a self-absorption that proves fatal—was spawned out of the same beliefs. "And still deeper the meaning of that story of Narcissus, who because he could not grasp the tormenting, mild image he saw in the fountain, plunged into it and was drowned," wrote Hermann Melville. "But that same image, we ourselves see in all rivers and oceans. It is the image of the ungraspable phantom of life; and this is the key to it all."

Classical Water Deities

Classical mythology incorporated a great deal of the preexisting pagan lore, constructing a highly complex religious system that, more than any other spiritual system, associated water with creation and destruction, fertility and death, beauty and sexuality, passion and power, and always with mystery. The deities chosen to symbolize these phenomena almost always appeared in an anthropomorphic form. They represented and controlled the forces of nature. The tension and attraction between these forces became the base of classical cosmology.

Oceanus, the son of Uranus (Heaven) and Gaea (Earth), for example, symbolized the great stream that, according to ancient geography, girded the earth. Ancient sages perceived it as the magnetic field around the earth that represented the oceanic possibilities of a world as yet unformed and

Edward Burne-Jones,
The Depths of the
Sea, *1887, watercolor
and gouache on paper
mounted on panel,
66⅝ x 29¾ in. (169.4
x 75.8 cm). Courtesy
of the Fogg Art Mu-
seum, Harvard Uni-
versity, Cambridge,
Massachusetts, Be-
quest of Grenville L.
Winthrop*

void, not unlike the waters of Genesis. In the human psyche Oceanus aroused the feelings of stupendous depth and vastness associated with the open sea—an experience of impersonal magnitude so intangible as to be frightening.

Oceanus and his sister/consort Tethys were Titans who ruled over the liquid element of a primordial world. When Zeus and his brothers overthrew the Titans, Poseidon succeeded Oceanus. His Roman counterpart, Neptune—originally a god of springs, a rather benign freshwater deity—gradually evolved into an awesome marine god associated with the tempestuous forces of water. Anthropomorphized as a fierce-looking, bearded warrior carrying a trident, he summoned or subdued storms. Horses with brazen hooves and golden manes drew his chariot over the sea, while the creatures of the deep frolicked around his path. He was the god of all waters and manipulated their ebb and flow.

Francesco Colonna, Neptune and the Horse, *miniature from a sixteenth-century vellum manuscript. Bibliothèque Nationale, Paris*

Nereids

Nereids, the beautiful and playful nymphs who graced the seas, were the daughters of Nereus, son of Oceanus, and Doris, his sister. They represented the harmony and balance of the waters and were sought by power-

ful forces. Neptune, for example, infatuated with the Nereid Amphitrite, courted her while riding on a dolphin. She was charmed. Having won her heart, Neptune made Amphitrite his wife and placed the magical dolphin, who brought them luck, among the stars.

The Nereid Thetis was so lovely that Zeus himself fell in love with her. But when Prometheus, a Titan, prophesied that she would bear a son who would someday become greater than his father, Zeus desisted and decreed that Thetis should be the wife of a mortal. King Peleus, with the help of Chiron, the centaur, won the Nereid's heart; their son became the Greek hero Achilles, who is also strongly associated with water.

The Nereid Galatea was not as fortunate as her sisters, because the Cyclops Polyphemus, who represented the dark and violent forces of the Homeric deep, obsessively pursued her. The Cyclops was so jealous that he destroyed Galatea's handsome young lover Acis by hurling an enormous boulder at him. At first, purple blood flowed out from under the rock that had felled Acis, but gradually it turned crystal clear. The rock cleaved open and the water uttered a soft murmur as it gushed from the chasm. Thus Acis was changed into a sacred river.

Leucothea was once a mortal woman named Ino who, fleeing with her little son from her evil husband Athamas, jumped off a cliff. Out of compassion, the gods saved their lives and gave them power over the forces of water deities, naming them Leucothea and Palaemon (Portunus). Leucothea was responsible for saving sailors from shipwreck, and Palaemon held jurisdiction over ports.

These myths inspired much poetry. Milton, for example, alludes to the idiosyncrasies of the entire hierarchy of the water deities in the song at the conclusion of *Comus:*

> . . . *Sabrina fair,*
> *Listen and appear to us.*
> *In name of great Oceanus;*
> *By the earth-shaking Neptune's mace,*
> *And Tethys' grave, majestic pace,*
> *By hoary Nereus' wrinkled look,*
> *And the Carpathian wizard's hook [Proteus]*
> *By scaly Triton's winding shell,*
> *And old soothsaying Glaucus' spell,*
> *By Leucothea's lovely hands,*
> *And her son who rules the strands.*
> *By Thetis' tinsel-slippered feet,*
> *And the songs of Sirens sweet.*

LEFT: *Andreas Groll,* Pan and the Nymphs, *1897 oil on canvas, 29½ × 43¼ in. (74.9 × 109.9 cm). Private collection*

FACING PAGE, TOP: *Sandro Botticelli,* The Birth of Venus, *ca. 1484–86, tempera on canvas, 67⅛ × 109⅞ in. (172.5 × 278.5 cm). Galleria degli Uffizi, Florence*

FACING PAGE, BOTTOM: *Aphrodite Poised on a Shell, third century B.C., sculpture. The Louvre, Paris*

Aphrodite

Perhaps the most seductive of the classical deities associated with water is Aphrodite (Venus), goddess of love and beauty and protectress of sailors. *Aphros* means "foam" and *Aphrodite* translates as "born of foam," because she was born from the sea foam of her father Uranus's severed erection. As early as 300 B.C. she was known by the epithet Anadyomene, "She who rises from the waves."

Rimbaud expressed his enormous passion for
Venus in Soleil et chair:

> How the earth is nubile and rich in blood;
> How its huge breast, raised by a soul,
> Is made of love, like God, and of flesh, like woman,
> And how it contains, big with sap and rays of light,
> The vast swarming of all embryos!
> And everything grows, and everything rises!
> —O Venus, O Goddess!

When weary of hunting, she returned to her grottos to
replenish herself with the sparkling waters of
her springs.

According to the myth, Uranus (Heaven) had been oppressing his wife Gaea (Earth), who encouraged their son Cronos to rebel against his father. Cronos castrated Uranus and scattered his father's seed over the ocean. The sperm, floating on the waves, became the sea foam from which the beautiful Aphrodite emerged in a scallop shell. Swept by gentle winds over the Aegean, she alighted on the island of Cyprus. So graceful and alluring was the goddess that the Seasons rushed to meet her, imploring her to stay.

This image of Aphrodite's birth lent itself to enormously rich visual representation. In paintings such as Botticelli's masterpiece *The Birth of Venus,* she appears naked, poised on a scallop shell, often in the *contrapposto* attitude. Aphrodite is forever linked to the white foamy sensuality of the sea, to the rhythm of the waves and the moisture of love. The marine animals connected with her also signify some aspect of sexual life. The scallop, for instance, pink-colored and tender, and lodged in a shell, clearly suggests the female genitalia. Aphrodite Pandemos, one of the earlier Greek forms of the goddess, was commonly depicted standing on a dolphin that represented joyous and playful eroticism. This earlier Aphrodite was also the goddess of vegetation, fecundity, and rain, as described by Aeschylus in *The Danaides:*

> The great and amorous sky curved over the earth, and lay upon her as a pure lover.
> The rain, the humid flux descending from heaven for both man and animal, for both thick and strong, germinated over wheat, swelled the furrows with fecund mud and brought forth the buds in the orchards. And it is I who empowered these moist espousals, I, the great Aphrodite.

In mythologies preceding the Olympians, Aphrodite was a fish deity with a great following in northern Syria and around Nineveh (which means "house of fish"). The anthropomorphic manifestation of the goddess came later. In the transformation, which is recorded on ancient Middle Eastern tablets, she is described as part maiden and part fish—a mermaid—and called Derketo. In *De Dea Syria* the Greek author Lucian described Derketo as a strange creature: "half was a woman, and from the thighs to the extremities of the feet, it appeared as the tail of a fish." Like her successor, she was born out of sea foam.

Ascalon, one of the most ancient temples ever to be excavated, exposed the fish cult of Atargatis, the Phrygian moon goddess, who was an earlier form of Aphrodite. Her splendid fish-tailed statue was covered with gems and gold, and the statues of sacred fish in her temples wore jewels in their fins, lips, and gills.

Artemis

Artemis—like her Roman counterpart, Diana—was the mistress of the soundless rivers and the umbrageous woods. Surrounded by her entourage of nymphs, she loved to haunt pools and cascading springs, occupying sacrosanct grottoes forbidden to everyone else. She represented the secretive part of the feminine psyche.

As rendered in Ovid's *Metamorphoses,* no mortal was ever to discover Diana's sacred cave, but one day Actaeon, king of Cadmus, chanced upon her as she was bathing, surrounded by a galaxy of naked nymphs. Spiritually unprepared for such a vision, the youth had such a lusty look in his eyes that Diana punished him by changing him into a stag. Actaeon was then pursued by his own hounds and shredded.

In earlier manifestations, Artemis/Diana also was a great fertility goddess identified with Selene, the moon. Her sacred grove in Nemi, near the Old Appian Way, was surrounded by waters that bubbled up from black rocks and fell in cascades into the lake. The poet Ovid, who often drank the water from this sacred spring, described the purling of the stream as it ran over the pebbles.

Egeria

Egeria, a water nymph, shared the grove in Nemi with Diana. Her lover was the Roman king Numa Pompilius, whose astute decisions were attributed to counsel from the nymph. The nuptials of Numa and Egeria were celebrated every May in the sacred grove of Nemi and were reminiscent of the sacred union between the powers of vegetation and water that occurred each spring to renew the fertility of the earth.

Egeria was also associated with healing. Plutarch described Egeria's spring gushing forth from a great oak tree. Its water was supposed to confer prophetic vision, and priestesses drew oracles from its murmurous flow. Within the sacred precinct of the spring, votive candles and small clay icons representing various parts of the human body have been discovered, suggesting that the waters had been used for healing. Many still believe this spring is endowed with miraculous attributes.

Water Nymphs

The ancients believed that the nymphs were supernatural powers associated with natural phenomena. They were divine spirits of woods, rivers, and mountain springs, and paragons of female youth and beauty. Under the appellations of naiads, oreads, dryads, and Nereids, they lived in caverns and grottoes, and sanctified springs, streams, lakes, and the sea. Naiads presided over brooks and fountains; oreads were nymphs of the mountains

Arnold Böcklin, Naiads at Play, *1886, oil on wood, 58⅞ x 41⅛ in. (149.5 x 104.5 cm). Oeffentliche Kunstsammlung Basel, Kunstmuseum/ Gottfried Keller Fund*

Paul Delvaux, Bathing Nymphs, *1938, oil on canvas, 51¼ x 59⅛ in. (130 x 150 cm). Private collection*

Collier Smithers, A Race of Mermaids and Tritons, 1895, oil on canvas, 40⅞ x 83 in. (104 x 211 cm). Whitford & Hughes, London

and grottoes; dryads presided over woods; and Nereids, as noted earlier, were sea nymphs. Spring and river nymphs brought nourishment to the earth, while sea nymphs saved pious navigators from shipwreck. All the nymphs were honored with prayer and sacrifice, and most mingled in love with favored mortals.

> *I regret the times of antiquated youth,*
> *Of lascivious satyrs, of animal fauns,*
> *The gods who bit of love's bough*
> *And in the rapids kissed the blond nymph.*
> RIMBAUD

As a result many heroes, such as the Greek Achilles, were descendants of a naiad or a Nereid.

Nymphs could represent sexual availability without anxiety. After all, they were more mortal than the higher deities. The freshwater nymphs were generally the devoted maidens of Artemis/Diana. But the sexually accessible nymphs, painted repeatedly by artists, were undoubtedly associates of Aphrodite who lacked her intimidating phallic penumbra.

Water nymphs appeared in Buddhist mythology as Acchara, celestial beings who inhabited the heaven of Sakka. They lived in a heavenly park and played their lutes to awaken the gods and goddesses so as to entertain them with their singing and dancing. Known also to seduce ascetics, they were often sent to earth as a form of punishment. In Islamic lore similar nymphs appeared in the form of houris, who also dwelled in heavenly pastures by magical streams and allured youths and brought vitality to old men.

Mermaids

Divine female power was often feared and associated with the seduction of mortal men, which could culminate in death and destruction. Mermaids, sirens, undines, ladies of the lake, and nixies presented both the life-threatening and the life-furthering aspects of water. They appeared as alluring and irresistible women without souls, who enticed unwary youths along riverbanks or the sea.

Esther Harding, a physician and specialist in the treatment of psychogenic illness, considers mermaids autoerotic: "They conquer men not only for love of the man, but to gain power over him. They cannot love, they can only desire. They are cold-blooded without human feeling or compassion. Instinct in its daemonic form, entirely non-human, lives through them. This unmediated living of instinct has a strangely attractive effect on men, it catches their attention and infatuation. Such women steal the man's soul, but they do not themselves experience the passion, the desire, the griefs of instinct. The lower part of the body is fish, not woman."

But mermaids were not always merciless; sometimes they guided lost ships home or warned sailors of impending danger; sometimes they even nursed men back to life. But ultimately they represented the inevitability and impossibility of interspecies union. H. G. Wells wrote a story about a

Edward Eriksen, The Little Mermaid, *1913, Copenhagen, bronze, 65 in. (165 cm).*

mermaid who fell in love with a mortal but could not love as a woman: all she could do was lure her lover into his grave. Hans Christian Andersen's mermaid had to give up her ability to speak in order to receive a pair of legs, a poignant symbol of sacrificing one's right of speech for acceptance.

But occasionally unions between mermaids and mortals were domestically satisfying and had happy endings. The sixteenth-century Swiss physician and alchemist Paracelsus professed that when a mermaid married a mortal and had a child, she received a soul.

Mermaids are still part of our contemporary mythology, appearing as benign little girls with fish tails and problems in children's stories and fairy tales, such as the book and film *The Little Mermaid,* but they also fire up the adult erotic imagination in such movies as *Million Dollar Mermaid* and *Splash.*

Sirens

Part woman and part bird, sirens were sea nymphs who lured mariners to destruction with their enchanting song. The power of their singing was so irresistible that in the *Odyssey* Circe instructed Ulysses to fill the ears of his sailors with wax, so they couldn't hear the sirens' seductive strains. She also warned him to tie himself to the mast and order his sailors not to release him until after they had left the sirens' island behind. Ulysses obeyed Circe's instructions. When his ship neared the island, the sea was calm and quiet. Over the silence drifted the strains of such seductive and mysterious music that Ulysses struggled with all his might to free himself and signaled to his crew to untie him. But they honored his initial command, tying him even tighter to the mast. The ship continued safely on its course and the music died away.

John William Waterhouse, Ulysses and the Sirens, *1891, oil on canvas, 39 x 79 in. (99 x 201 cm). National Gallery of Victoria, Melbourne*

*Wright Barker,
Circe, 1890s, oil on
canvas, 54¼ x 78¼ in.
(138 x 199.5 cm).
Bradford Art Gal-
leries & Museums,
England*

The Neck

Everywhere the impending danger of water was lurking. In Celtic mythology, waters were infested with sprites and monsters. The Icelandic Nikr, from which the colloquial term "Old Nick" may derive—was popularly perceived as the devil. There were many manifestations of the ancient Nikr: the beautiful nixie who allured young fishermen and sailors to seek her embraces in the waves that drowned them; the river sprite known as the Neck, who seized and drowned maidens who played upon his banks; the German river spirit who annually demanded tribute of human life.

The Neck appeared in various forms: as a beautiful little boy with golden ringlets, wearing a red cap; as a handsome young man from the waist up and a horse below; and sometimes as an old man with a long beard, sitting on a cliff and wringing the water out of his beard, resembling the Scandinavian god Odin.

A great musician, the Neck was often seen sitting by the water playing his golden harp, the harmonious sounds of which influenced all nature. Because he was unpredictable and put spells on people who passed by, peasants feared him and tried "to bind the Neck," using metals, especially steel, while singing out the charm:

> *Neck, neck, nail in water!*
> *The virgin Mary casteth steel in water!*
> *Do you sink, I flit!*

Lord Frederic Leighton, The Bath of Psyche, *1890 (exhibited), oil on canvas, 74½ x 24½ in. (189.2 x 66.2 cm). Tate Gallery, London*

Bruce Chatwin's In Patagonia *cites the story of an American explorer named Martin Sheffield: "in the middle of the lake, I saw the head of an animal. At first sight it was like some unknown species of swan, but swirls in the water made me think its body must resemble a crocodile's." What followed was an extensive and expensive monster search that resulted in nothing.*

Water Monsters

A universal myth that spreads from Japan and Annam in the East to Senegambia, Scandinavia, and Scotland in the West involves a many-headed serpent or dragon that threatens to destroy the people of a given land unless a human victim, usually a virgin, is delivered to him periodically. Almost always a young man of humble descent slays the monster, saves the land, marries the virgin, and inherits the kingdom.

One such hero was Perseus. As a punishment for his wife's obsessive boasting, Cepheus, king of Joppa, was instructed by the sea nymphs to offer his daughter Andromeda to a many-headed sea monster. Perseus, who had recently decapitated the Gorgon Medusa, pitied the terrified maiden

Lord Frederic Leighton, Perseus and Andromeda, *1891 (reworked 1894), oil on canvas, 92½ x 50⅞ in. (235 x 129.2 cm). Courtesy of the Board of Trustees of the National Museums and Galleries on Merseyside; Walker Art Gallery, Liverpool*

chained on a rock waiting to be devoured. He volunteered to slay the monster if he could have her for his wife. Everyone agreed, and the young hero pounced upon the monster's back and plunged his sword into it. A violent struggle ensued, but Perseus succeeded in giving the monster a fatal stroke. Andromeda's parents rejoiced, and the virgin descended from the rock and married the victor.

Another legend involves Hercules, who earned the name "water tamer." The people of Argos were being terrorized by the Hydra, a nine-headed monster that inhabited a mineral spring in the nearby marshes of Lerna. The spring would bubble black water, then suddenly the monster would leap out spewing venom and devour anyone in sight. If one of the Hydra's heads was cut off, two others grew in its place. But Hercules managed to decapitate the Hydra completely, thus taming the raging waters of the spring into a single channel.

In the myth of Psyche and Eros, Aphrodite as a punishment orders Psyche to bring her the Waters of Life. She gives Psyche a crystal vessel and instructs her to fill it with water from the underworld rivers, which flow from the highest crags of an enormous mountain guarded by dragons. Psyche is aided by Zeus's eagle, who informs her that the task is impossible even for the gods. Nonetheless, the good eagle flies off with the vessel, dodges the dragons, fills the vessel with the Waters of Life, and brings it back to Psyche.

The Loch Ness Monster

Water monsters transcend all cultural and geographical boundaries, as they have been alleged to exist in nearly every ocean and lake in the world. They range from giant fish-giraffes to hundred-foot-long tadpoles to giant octopuses. As recently as 1989, a group of Philippine fishermen claimed that their boat was capsized by a giant octopus.

Scottish and Irish folklore is filled with stories of kelpies, or water horses, that live in various lochs. As a Scottish ballad relates:

> *The side was steep, the bottom deep*
> *Frae bank to bank the water pouring;*
> *And the bonnie lass did quake for fear,*
> *She heard the water-kelpie roaring.*

Although many of these monsters, such as Grendel in *Beowulf* or the creature in *The Creature from the Black Lagoon,* are literary creations, others are part of our shared reality. The Loch Ness monster is probably the most famous of the monsters inhabiting lakes and rivers around the world. "Nessie," as it is affectionately called, is usually described as black or brown in color, twenty to thirty feet long, with a small horselike head on a long neck, small horns, a thick body that can contract into humps, and at least two flippers.

The Loch Ness Mon-
ster(¿), 1934.

"If it were not that an otter swimming seems a very large creature, I would hardly know what to think of it," wrote Sir Walter Scott in a letter, "for a very cool-headed, sensible man told me he had seen it in broad daylight—he scouted my idea of an otter and said the animal was more like a cow or a horse."

Rumors of creatures in Loch Ness go as far back as the sixth century. St. Columba, an Irish missionary who Christianized Scotland, was once standing at the edge of Loch Ness while a man was swimming nearby. Suddenly a monster rose up out of the water; the swimmer was terrified, but St. Columba drove the beast away with the sign of the cross and a sharp command not to touch the swimmer.

Whereas the St. Columba story depicts a threatening monster, recent accounts portray the Loch Ness monster as peaceful and shy. It has become evident, however, that there cannot be just one creature (otherwise it would now be some thirteen hundred years old), but perhaps a colony of plesiosaurs, small dinosaurs related to the modern turtle, that have survived from the age of reptiles. But the elusiveness of the creature has prompted paranormal or psychic explanations of its existence. It seems to belong to the realm of ghosts and angels.

Till taught by pain
Men really know not what good water's worth.
If you had been in Turkey or in Spain,
Or with a famished boat's crew had your berth,
Or in the desert heard the camel's bell,
You'd wish yourself where truth is—in a well.

LORD BYRON

Rites

Rainmaking

Rain is the lifegiver, the sustainer of all living beings on earth. It makes things grow. Without rain, vegetation withers, animals and people languish and die.

To the ancient Hebrews rain was a blessing from heaven granted in return for obeying the Law. Its source was thought to be a great reservoir of water in heaven; God controlled the faucet. Although drought was caused by sin, retribution was not impossible, as is illustrated by the story of drought and famine in the land of Ahab (1 Kings: 18), in which God promises rain to the prophet Elijah if the people will turn their hearts from the evil god Baal. The people do as God wishes, whereupon a little cloud appears and it rains.

Since rain was considered a gift from heaven, people devised ways of pleasing the divinities who controlled the skies. Even though these complex magic and religious rituals varied dramatically around the world, their purpose was always the same: to attract the attention of the deities, thank them, invite their pity, and persuade them to keep the celestial waters flowing.

Walter Shirlaw,
Dawn, 1886, oil on
canvas, 66 x 33 in.
(167.6 x 83.8 cm).
Private collection

Rain Dancing

One time when Black Raven was living on earth, it rained for so long that
everything he owned got wet. His clothes and provisions began to rot. His un-
derground house filled with water. At last, he said to his eldest son, Emmem-
qut, "Universe must be doing something up there, let's fly up and see." They
went outside, put on their raven coats, and flew to the Universe's place, where
they heard the sound of the drum from within. It was Universe who was drum-
ming. His wife, Rain Woman, was beside him. He had cut off her vulva and
hung it on the drum. He had also cut off his penis and was using it as a drum-
stick. When he beat the drum, water poured from the vulva as rain.

Ancient myth

And so the sacred ritual of beating the vulva with a penis to bring on the
forces of rain and fertility came into being.

Music and dance have long been an important part of rainmaking rituals. Native American tribes perform visionary rain dances, and their rainmakers are their shamans. I had the privilege of attending such a ceremony
among the Pueblo. With tenacity, grace, and dignity the dancers withstood
the midsummer heat until it began to pour.

The entire community, including the children, participated in these rituals, which went on for hours, sometimes days, until the dancing and
chanting brought on a rhythmic, trancelike state. Through such intense collective exhilaration, tribal peoples believed they could reach the powers
of rain.

Homeopathic Magic

The spiritual leaders whose task was to intercede between the humans and
the gods to negotiate rain became known as the rainmakers—usually the
most respected, wise, and powerful figures in their tribe or community.
Their invocations were often based on homeopathic, or imitative, magic:
they mimicked the effect they wanted to produce. In parts of India, for
instance, the rainmaker sprinkled water on the earth, pretending to be a
cloud. Buddhist priests induced rain by filling small holes in the temple
floor with water, symbolizing the earth's acceptance of rain.

In a village near Dorpat in Russia, three men would climb up a tree in a
sacred fir grove. One of them would drum on a kettle to simulate thun-
der, the second would create sparks by rubbing firebrands together to imi-
tate lightning, and the third would dip twigs into a container of water and
sprinkle it in all directions so as to mimic rain.

In Walachia and among the Romanians and Transylvanians, a girl would
be crowned with the last ears of corn and everyone would throw water on
her to ensure an abundant crop the following year. This practice is still
carried out—even in certain parts of the United States. In Prussia, when
plowmen and sowers returned home from the fields, the women would

splash them with water. In return, they would throw the women in a pond and dunk them, so as to make sure that the seeds they had sown would not perish from drought.

In southern India, women tied live frogs to winnowing fans and sang songs about the frogs' need for water. Other participants sprinkled water over the frogs; rain was supposed to follow in torrents.

In various cultures frogs, snakes, salamanders, and turtles were considered protégés of the rain god and custodians of rain. Other animals were thought to forecast rain. In Ireland, for example, the cry of the curlew signals rain. Ants scurrying to their hills also indicate rain, as do crows, wild geese, swallows, gnats, or lightning bugs flying low. In Nova Scotia, mosquitos bite most fiercely just before it rains. In Newfoundland, if a cat drowns in the sea, it is sure to rain. It will also rain if you kill a toad, frog, or spider.

Magic Rituals

Endless symbols were used and sacrifices made to bring on rain. Among the Angoni and Baronga in Africa, ribald songs were chanted, often by twins. In the Caucasus, young girls yoked themselves to a plow and hauled it to the arid riverbed. In Transylvania, virgins sat naked on a harrow and prayed. The Arunta in Australia constructed votive rainbows over dead snakes.

The Aymara Indians near Lake Titicaca on the Peru-Bolivia border still observe a rainmaking ritual in which their shaman, Paqo, goes in his balsa to the lake and fills several basins with water, frogs, and certain water plants. Musicians in other balsas follow him, playing panpipes and drums. Paqo, the musicians, and a mixed chorus of men and women then climb Atoja Mountain and put the plants and frogs on altars, as offerings to the spirits of the deep. Paqo prays to the mountain spirits, Father and Mother Atoja, and the chorus sings the frog song. The sun disappears and rain begins to pour.

Among the Greeks in Thessaly and Macedonia, a procession of children, led by a girl adorned with flowers, would be sent to springs and wells to make a plea for rain. Every time the procession stopped, the children would drench the leading girl with a bucket of water while singing an invocation:

> *Perperia all fresh bedewed,*
> *Freshen all the neighborhood*
> *By the woods, on the highway,*
> *As thou goest, to God now pray:*
> *O my God, upon the plain,*

Send thou still, small rain,
That the fields may fruitful be,
And vines in blossom we may see;
That the grain be full and sound,
And wealthy grow the folks around.

Similarly, Serbians would strip a young girl naked and cover her entire body and face with a mantle of leaves, flowers, and herbs. They called her Dodola. Accompanied by other girls, she danced through the village, leaping and whirling, while the rest formed a ring around her and sang:

We go through the village;
The clouds go in the sky;
We go faster,
Faster go the clouds;
They have overtaken us,
And wetted the corn and the vine.

Afterward a housewife would pour water over Dodola to complete the ceremony.

Moon Goddesses and Vestal Virgins

Based on their observation of weather conditions for centuries, farmers and sailors deduced that the weather varied according to the phases of the moon. Rainmaking ceremonies were often closely related to the moon's phases, too. In the early agrarian societies, women were experts in sowing

Meinrad Craighead, Moon Tree, 1983, ink painting on scratchboard, 10 x 10 in. (25.4 x 25.4 cm). Collection of Alice Saunders, North Carolina

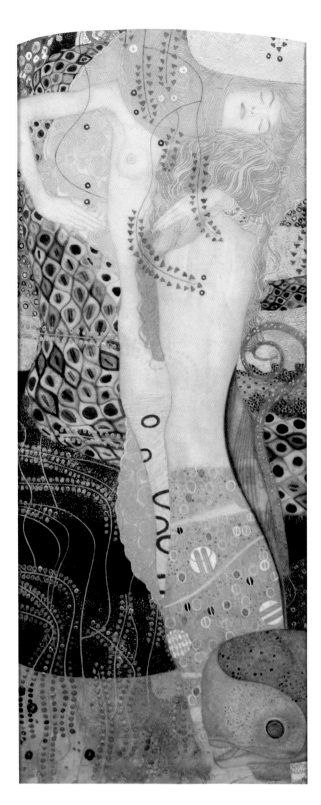

Gustav Klimt, Bisce
d'Acqua, *1904–7,
oil on parchment, 19⅝
x 7⅞ in. (50 x 20 cm).
Österreichische
Galerie, Vienna*

Ancient Germanic tribes believed
that women were holy and consulted
them as oracles. These holy women
looked at the swirling rivers,
listened to their murmur, and made
prophecies.

seeds, raising crops, tending animals, and other agricultural tasks. They also had a special biological connection to the moon and its phases. Because of this, they played an important part in rainmaking ceremonies.

These primitive rites usually had the double function of venerating the moon goddess as giver of rain and encouraging her moisture-giving powers. Pouring water to induce the goddess to send rain was an extreme sacrifice at times when water was scarce.

Women often performed rainmaking rites naked. They gathered the necessary herbs and cleaned out the springs as part of the ritual. Then they sprinkled themselves with fresh water and went around pouring water over the graves of their ancestors in secret groves.

In the village of Ploska in Russia, women of all ages went naked to the boundaries of the village at night and poured water on the ground. This was also performed as a solitary ritual by a girl—the candidate for priestess of the moon diety, whose most important functions were taking care of the water supply and tending the sacred flame.

In Peru the priestesses of Mam-Quilla were vestal virgins and also rainmakers. In ancient Rome six vestals, guardians of the sacred fire of Vesta, performed a ceremony during the full moon on the Ides of May to regulate the water supply. This ritual included throwing twenty-four manikins into the Tiber. At one time humans had been sacrificed to achieve the same result. In parts of Europe, effigies of Death and Carnival are still thrown into rivers.

One exception to women's omnipotence in rainmaking rituals was found among the Abkhaz in the western Caucasus. Women were not only excluded from rainmaking rituals but were not even supposed to utter the name of Afi, the god of rain and thunderstorms. They simply referred to him as "the one who is above."

Rituals of Isis and Osiris

Much of Christian water symbolism was gleaned from the cult of Isis and Osiris, the moon deities of ancient Egypt. This cult spread throughout the Roman Empire and at one time had as many followers as Christianity. The Egyptians celebrated the union of Isis and Osiris in the annual procession of Phallephoria. They carried a bowl of water, symbolizing the fertilizing moisture as well as the power of the moon, in front of an image of an erect phallus. Year after year the mysteries were revealed through these icons of regeneration: the bowl, which was Isis, the mother, the vessel of life; and the phallus, the fertilizing power of Osiris. Those who understood the mysteries had the chance to participate in a life that was renewed like the ancient and eternal moon.

Osiris, husband and brother of Isis, was trapped in a chest by his evil brother Set and thrown into the Nile. Isis went in search of her beloved, but in vain. Osiris's chest became entangled in the reeds near the shores of Byblos, where a tree growing in the marsh wound its trunk around the god's coffin. This beautiful tree was cut down and became a pillar in the palace of the king of Phoenicia. Isis posed as a servant and reclaimed the coffin. But this time Set dismembered Osiris into fourteen parts and threw them into the river. Isis was able to retrieve all the parts except the phallus, which had been consumed by a fish. She put all the pieces together and, through her divine sorcery, fashioned a golden phallus, upon which she lay, conceiving their child Horus. Afterward she buried Osiris's parts at Philae in Egypt, which became a center of pilgrimages.

Ablution

Hector Leroux, Sacrarium, 1889, photogravure, 12 x 8 in. (30.5 x 20.3 cm). Collection of the author

Ablution, the washing away of sins or impurities, was initially associated with the mysteries of Eleusis, a city in ancient Greece where sacred rites called mysteries were performed. These ceremonies began with a lustration in the sea. "To the sea, ye mystics!" the leader of the festivities would cry, and the initiates would plunge into the water, from which they emerged new people with new names.

Consecrated water has long served for purification and spiritual cleansing of people and objects in most parts of the world. Aztec midwives, for example, would chant, "May this water purify and quieten thy heart: may it wash all that is evil," as they bathed the infants they had delivered into the world. This custom calls to mind the Rites of the First Bath for the newborn imperial baby, perhaps the first ablution to be codified in Japanese history. Complete with ceremonies and a reading of the scriptures, this ritual is also reminiscent of Christian baptism—although its practice is restricted to the Japanese imperial family.

Women making offerings during the Festival of Chait (the sun god) in Janakpur, Nepal.

In Janakpur, Nepal, known for its many ponds (there are 108), during the festival of the sun god Chait, which takes place every November or December, women line the ponds with offerings. At dusk they immerse themselves waist-deep into the water and hold the offerings up to the setting sun. At dawn they return and perform the same ceremony to the rising sun. As they stand in the ponds, they pray to the sun god for favors or give thanks for those already granted. In the past they used to stay in the ponds all night as a kind of penance.

Sacred Disinfectant

Worshipers of the Egyptian Isis used water as a sacred disinfectant. Their priests and priestesses had water poured over their hands and heads before beginning a ritual, and the people imitated them. Old reliefs depict priests performing similar ablution rituals on corpses.

Washing of the dead in all cultures symbolized purification of the soul before it entered the afterworld. Peruvians believed that their ancestors suffered a thirst peculiar to the dead and offered water during funerals both to cleanse the dead and to quench their thirst.

The Hebrew fathers raised cleanliness to a moral precept, declaring, "Cleanliness is next to godliness." Before approaching a tabernacle, rabbis had to wash their hands and feet. *Mikvahs*, or ritual baths, were established by Orthodox Jews for cleansing and purifying themselves, especially before sacred events. Likewise, when Orthodox and Catholic Christians enter their churches, they dip their fingers in holy water and make the sign of the cross. The Islamic custom of taking ablutions before entering a mosque evolved out of a similar respect for cleanliness before praying to Allah.

During the Middle Ages, spiritual cleansing was practiced among the Celts in the form of a quick plunge in cold water. On the eve of his knighthood, a squire would be escorted by two "esquires of honor brave" to a barber, who shaved his beard and trimmed his hair. Then he was taken to a bath and doused with cold water. After this ritual bath, the knights of the court would lead him to the chapel, where spiced wine was served and minstrels sang throughout the night. At sunrise he was knighted.

Mosaic of the Nile, first century B.C., portion of the floor mosaic from the Temple of Fortuna, Palestrina. Museo Archeologico Prenestino

Baptism

"He also went into the water for baptism from whom Adam received his features," writes Wolfram von Eschenbach in *Parcival.*

Christian baptism has its roots in Egyptian rituals, Greek catharsis, and Shinto, Confucian, and Hindu customs such as bathing in the Ganges. Since water played a conspicuous part in Midsummer Day rites, the Christian Church chose to throw its cloak over this heathen festival and dedicate it to St. John the Baptist. The plunge bath, which remained an important part of Judaism, became the Christian baptismal bath of transformation.

Christians came to believe no one can enter the kingdom of heaven without baptism by water. Although early baptismal rituals were performed in "living water," water flowing from springs and rivers, baptisms eventually moved indoors; the baptismal font (a word derived from the Latin *fons,* meaning "fountain" or "spring" as well as designating the god of springs) replaced the living water.

During Easter, the solemn blessing of the water for baptism prepares it for its great task of renewing souls. A culminating point is reached when the Easter candle symbolizing Christ is submerged in the water and raised up again, representing Christ lowered into the grave and rising from it. As the burning candle is about to be lowered into the water, the celebrant utters the words: "May a heavenly offspring, conceived in holiness and reborn into a new creation, come forth from the stainless womb of this divine font."

This custom resembles the Isis and Osiris ritual of the vessel and the phallus, in that the holy font of baptism is "fertilized" by the lighted candle. Thus the water becomes the symbol of both death and life: death to sin and spiritual rebirth. The priest's prayer blessing the baptismal water expresses all the spiritual significance of water:

> *In baptism we use your gift of water,*
> *which you have made a rich symbol*
> *of the grace you give us in this sacrament.*
>
> *At the very dawn of creation*
> *your spirit breathed on the waters,*
> *making them the wellspring of all holiness.*
>
> *The waters of the great flood*
> *you made a sign of the waters of baptism,*
> *that make an end of sin and a new beginning of goodness.*
>
> *Through the waters of the Red Sea*
> *you led Israel out of slavery,*
> *to be an image of God's holy people,*
> *set free from sin by baptism.*

In the waters of Jordan
your Son was baptized by John
and anointed with the Spirit.

Your Son willed that water and blood
should flow from his side
as he hung upon the cross.

After his resurrection he told his disciples:
"Go out and teach all nations,
baptizing them in the name of the Father
and the Son and of the Holy Spirit."

Father, look now with love upon thy Church,
and unseal for her the fountain of baptism.

By the power of the Spirit
give to the water of this font
the grace of your Son.

You created man in your own likeness:
cleanse him from sin in a new birth of innocence
by water and the Spirit.
[The priest lowers the Easter candle into the water either
once or three times as he continues:]
We ask you, Father, with your Son
to send the Holy Spirit upon the waters of this font.
[He holds the candle in the water.]
May all who are buried with Christ
in the death of baptism
rise also with him to newness of life.
We ask this through Christ our Lord. Amen.
[The candle is taken out of the water as the people sing:]
Springs of water, bless the Lord.
Give him glory and praise for ever.

Those who are to be baptized then renounce the devil individually, are questioned about their faith, and are baptized.

One manifestation of Christ's transcendence—his ability to walk on water—has its roots in earlier pagan traditions, probably those of the Celtic druids. Purity of soul is the criterion for being able to tread on water. We see a modern example of this in Jerzy Kosinski's novel Being There, *at the end of which protagonist Chauncey Gardner performs the same miracle.*

O ship, new billows are carrying
you out to sea. Where are you going?
Struggle to reach port.
HORACE, *Odes 1.14*

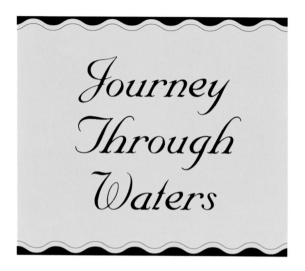

Journey Through Waters

The Hero's Journey

The invention of the boat made possible a fluid mobility through waters that would greatly expand the consciousness of the human race. The depth and vastness of the seas and rivers summoned the human spirit. Not only did waterways present the possibility of great commerce and communication, but they also became a channel for the pursuit of self-knowledge, a place where people confronted their fears and passions. And if, like Ulysses, the traveler managed to return home, he had to redefine reality in a new context.

Homer's *Odyssey* is the quintessential sea voyage. The hero is so driven with rashness and arrogance that nothing will stand in his way. In canto 26 of the *Divine Comedy*, Dante compares Ulysses' voyage to original sin. "Neither fondness for my son nor reverence for my aged father, nor the due love that should have cheered Penelope could conquer in me the ardour that I had to gain experience of the world, of human vice and worth," the hero says, confessing his obsession.

A hero's journey through unknown and dangerous waters is one of the greatest metaphors in literature, art, myth, and dreams. Presenting different aspects of personal confrontation and realization, it becomes a paradigm for the journey of life itself. The restlessness of the sea represents the rest-

John William Whiteley, A Sail (Ulysses and the Sirens), 1898, oil on canvas, 55 x 69 in. (139.7 x 175.3 cm). Private collection

lessness of the hero. The sea is a challenge, a necessary evil to confront, a crossing that separates and estranges. It also brings tremendous loneliness and alienation, as expressed in Coleridge's *Rime of the Ancient Mariner:*

Alone, alone, all, all alone
alone on a wide wide sea!

Forbidding Waters

For the Western mind, the sea was terrifying and forbidding. "The sea or the great waters, that is, are the symbol for the primordial undifferentiated flux, the substance that created nature only by having form imposed upon or wedded to it," wrote W. H. Auden in *The Enchafèd Flood.* "The sea, in fact," he continues, "is that state of barbaric vagueness and disorder out of which civilization has emerged and into which, unless saved by the effort of gods and men, it is liable to relapse. It is so little a friendly symbol that the first thing that the author of the Book of Revelation notices in his vision of the new heaven and earth at the end of time is that 'there was no more sea.'"

The Chinese philosopher Lao-tzu presents an opposing point of view in chapter 8 of *Tao te Ching:* "Water is peaceful and extends its beneficent action throughout Nature, not even disdaining those gloomy depths which the vulgar look upon with horror, for water works much as God does."

Water can both float and sink a ship.

Chinese proverb

J.M.W. Turner,
Wreckers—Coast
of Northumber-
land, with a Steam
Boat Assisting a
Ship off Shore,
*1834, oil on canvas,
35⅝ x 47½ in. (90.4
x 120.7 cm). Yale
Center for British Art,
New Haven, Con-
necticut, Paul Mellon
Collection*

Exploring the Depths

Exploring the depths of the sea is another metaphor for searching the interior limits of the psyche and diving into the darkest realms of the unknown.
Modern-day explorers like Jacques Cousteau have committed themselves
to exploring the mystery in those depths, and Greenpeace, the radical environmental organization, enforces moral principles in its heroic attempt to
preserve endangered sea mammals.

The depths of the sea are also perceived as a metaphor for indepen-
dence from earthly values:

> *The sea does not belong to despots. Upon its surface men can still exercise
> unjust laws, fight, tear one another to pieces, and be carried away with ter-
> restial horrors. But at thirty feet below its level, their reign ceases, their influ-
> ence is quenched, and their power disappears. Ah, sir; live, live in the bosom of
> the waters. There is only independence. There I recognize the master's voice.
> There I'm free.*

Captain Nemo in Jules Verne's
Twenty Thousand Leagues Under the Sea

Sailors considered it a bad omen to have a woman aboard, expecting
her to bring destruction because she would make the sea jealous. Women
appeared only along the way—on islands and rocks or in grottoes—either
as fatal temptations in the form of sirens or mermaids, or as refuge in the
form of a good witch like Calypso.

The sea represents the uncontrolled side of the Great Goddess; she appears in her most malevolent aspects at sea, in the form of the sea witch, the siren, or the mermaid. These are the dark areas that men are compelled to explore. She frequently appears in literature as well as mythology, becoming the castrating white whale in *Moby Dick* or Life-in-Death to the Ancient Mariner:

> *Her lips were red, her looks were free,*
> *Her locks were yellow as gold;*
> *Her skin was white as leprosy . . .*

Although "sea" is feminine in many languages, the sea voyage is almost always a masculine journey. Women themselves found the sea alien. "It is human nature to stand in the middle of a thing," wrote Marianne Moore, referring to the ocean, "but you cannot stand in the middle of this." Crossing the great waters was inappropriate for women. The American author Robert Johnson comments that the feminine way of taking the elixir of life from a fast-moving, treacherous river is one drop at a time.

Why is the spectacle of the sea so infinitely and eternally agreeable? Because the sea presents at once the idea of immensity and of movement . . . twelve or fourteen leagues of liquid in movement are enough to convey to man the highest expression of beauty which he can encounter in his transient abode.

CHARLES BAUDELAIRE, *Mon coeur mis à nu*

River Quests

In most mythologies female deities journey on the rivers, searching for someone they have lost or a part of themselves they hope to retrieve. This is a quest not for self but for a missing part. Isis looking for Osiris, Psyche for Eros, and Ishtar for Tammuz represent the journey in search of the other half, according to the Platonic ideal. It is a quest for perfection, harmony, and wholeness on earth.

Henrietta Rae, Psyche Before the Throne of Venus, 1894, 29⅞ x 47¼ in. (76 x 120 cm). Arthur Fish, Henrietta Rae, General Research Division, New York Public Library, Astor, Lenox and Tilden Foundations

In the myth of Psyche and Eros, water plays an important role. Psyche has lost her love, Eros, as a punishment for disobedience, and she is given difficult tasks by Aphrodite, her beloved's mother, in order to get him back. We have already seen how Psyche, befriended by the eagle of Zeus, was able to bring the Waters of Life to Aphrodite. Another of Aphrodite's challenging tasks is to gather the wool of a herd of sheep with golden fleece grazing near a river. As Psyche sets out, she is in such despair that she throws herself in the river, but a singing reed befriends her and reveals the secret of obtaining the fleece. The reed represents fate with its impeccable sense of timing.

Growth was the expected result from the sea journey, and a few continents were discovered along the way. The river journey, in contrast, emphasized the process.

I walk to the river's bank before the night
to stand and watch there for a passing minute.
My soul has something of the water in it
that I should be so lifted by the sight.

The dark creeps out of bush and fern and glen,
as if to make that lovely mirror blind.
But see: the early stars are out and find
themselves below me and shine back again.
                    HERMANN CLAUDIUS, *Water*

River and Flood Myths

Sacred Rivers

As a child, I once saw an atlas that had a map labeled "The Great Rivers of the World." It listed strange names, like ancient incantations, that I was compelled to memorize. They formed a language of their own: Mississippi, Missouri, Amazon, Tigris, Euphrates, Congo, Niger, Nile, Volga, Ganges, Yukon, Dnieper, Dniester, Loire, Saskatchewan, Indus, Hwang, Yangtze, Mekong, Danube, Zambezi, Colorado, and Rio Grande. I know there were many more —sinuous blue lines on a map devoid of geological indications and boundaries, each line meandering through invisible mountains and valleys, always seeking the sea. As an African proverb reminds us, "Water may flow in a thousand channels but it all returns to the sea."

The great rivers of the world are evolutionary miracles. What makes them extraordinary is that they have been tamed by time; history has flowed through their waters. They have witnessed a multitude of civilizations and become a matrix of memory safeguarding our primordial secrets, a bard transmitting old stories, with ritualistic and psychic access to the invisible world.

"Water fills up all the empty places on the earth and clings fast to it," says Lao-tzu. And when the empty places are filled, it overflows to create new ones to fill, drenching anything in its path.

Elliot Daingerfield,
The Forest Pool,
1915, oil on canvas,
24 x 28 in. (61 x
71.1 cm). Private
collection

Our evolution undoubtedly was driven by our need to migrate in search of water. Prehistoric humans were always seeking temperate climates that yielded fertile lands and an abundance of water. As their numbers grew, they migrated farther, seeking ever greater water sources. Once they found them, they invented creative ways of domesticating water. Nomads settled on the land; they irrigated fields, built channels, diverted rivers. They transformed the land into fertile fields and planted seeds.

From mud, they made jugs, urns, and other vessels; they also made bricks for building houses and temples. Flint weapons were shaped into shovels and hoes, as communities became disenchanted with the unpredictable and endless search for game and wild plants. Clans grew quickly into tribes, and tribes developed into villages, towns, cities, and eventually city-states.

Four thousand years ago the rulers of Assyria converted the sterile valley between the Tigris and Euphrates rivers into the Fertile Crescent, the cradle of Western civilization. They created immense artificial lakes for conserving the flood waters and devised great canals for irrigation and transportation. The Nahrawan Canal, for instance, supplied by the waters

Sacred waterfall on the island of Kosamui off the coast of Thailand.

of the Tigris, was over four hundred miles long and four hundred feet wide, with sufficient depth for navigation by the vessels of that time.

The rulers of these communities were the masters of water. Rivers were their treasure and the source of their physical and spiritual existence. As such, their rivers were treated with great respect and reverence. They kept them clean and offered them sacrifices to express their gratitude. They built their holy sites along the rivers. The sanctuaries and temples of the great Assyrian city of Assur, for example, stretched along the Tigris. The Egyptians, as we know, built theirs along the Nile. The reservoir of Lake Moeris in Egypt was the largest in the Nile Valley and supported twenty million people.

The Nile

For the ancient Egyptians, the Hellenistic Greeks, and the Romans, Nile water was sacred—especially the floodwater, which represented the "re-birthing" of the river. The springtime flood was perceived as a holy gift; the water flowed onto the land, regenerating it and providing fertility.

"Thou are the waterer of the fields which Ra had created," sang the Egyptians to their river. "Thou givest life unto all animals, thou makest all the land to drink unceasingly as thou descendest on thy way from heaven."

They celebrated the overflow as a cleansing of the spirit as well. The greatest tribute one could render a god was to be drowned in the river and consequently unite with him. In Egyptian, the word for "drown" originally meant "praise."

As far back as 330 B.C. in Pharaonic and Ptolemaic times, Egyptians were constructing nilometers, enormous crypts under temples to measure the rise and fall of the river and to symbolically re-create the flood. The nilometers were intended primarily to provide pure Nile water for the liturgical needs of the Isis-Serapis cult. Not only did they simulate floods but they also acted as hosts to real floods during the rainy season.

The Niger

The Nupe of Nigeria tell how the Niger River was formed: The king of the Nupe, northern neighbors of the Yoruba, consulted the oracle Ifa on how to prevent an enemy invasion. Ifa told him to get some black cloth and let a virgin tear it. The king gave the cloth to his own daughter Oya, who tore it and flung the two pieces to the ground. In front of everyone's eyes, the cloth turned into black water, flowing from the nucleus of the kingdom.

The Ijaw believe that their river, the Niger, transmits psychic information without profanely disclosing it. On New Year's Eve people bathe in the lower delta and collectively dream of water spirits and underwater voyages. They also believe that, during the flood, water spirits are swept into their villages. When the flood recedes, it gets rid of their accumulated sins. In the

*Tosa Mitsutada,
Lovers (page from
The Tale of Genji
album), 1894. The
Metropolitan
Museum of Art, New
York, Gift of Mary L.
Cassilly, 1894.
94.18.1h*

past, a human scapegoat used to carry these sins in a canoe-shaped vessel on his head until the cleansing flood pulled him into the ocean and swept him away.

River Pilgrimages

Some rivers have become sacred because of their association with holy people or their healing faculties. Christians from all over the world, for example, make pilgrimages to the River Jordan, where Jesus was baptized.

Hindus believe that the sixty thousand sons of King Sagara were punished with incineration for their arrogance. The divine goddess Ganga was brought down from the heavens to purify their ashes. She performed this rite at the delta of the Bay of Bengal, and the river was named after her. Ever since, Hindus have paid homage to the Ganges, believing that all sin is instantly cleansed away by a ritual bath in the river. And those who are drowned in it are reborn among the gods.

The boats discovered in ancient Japanese tombs had been placed there to transport the souls of the dead to the afterlife.

Arthur Durston, The Flood, *1936, oil on canvas, 30 x 36 in. (76.2 x 91.4 cm). Private collection*

Mythical Rivers

Rivers have not only spawned mythology, some exist only *in* mythology. In classical mythology, for example, hell had five rivers: Styx, Acheron, Cocytus, Phlegethon, and Lethe. The Styx, sometimes known as the river of hate, flowed nine times around the infernal regions, and the ferryman, Charon, took passengers across to Hades. Contact with the waters of the

Styx endowed mortals with supernatural skills. Achilles' mother, Thetis, for example, had dipped him in the Styx when he was an infant, making him invulnerable except for the heel by which she held him. The River Lethe caused oblivion, making the dead souls forget their former lives.

The concept of the river as the connector of life and death is universal. In parts of West Africa, people hold the belief that the dead are canoed across three rivers separating this world from the other one. Sometimes the Yoruba, an inland people, bury their dead in canoes to prepare them for their journey upon a mythical river.

Buddha used the metaphors of the Big Ferry and the Little Ferry to teach his followers about the journey to nirvana. Buddhists and Taoists alike embrace the concept of "crossing the great waters," but add a hitch by asserting that "no one can cross the same river twice."

The Great Deluge

The flood is probably the world's oldest metaphor; it represents the power of both good and evil as well as the destruction of an old world and the birth of a new one. In the story of the flood, destruction becomes purification and renewal; death leads to rebirth.

The greatest ablution of the earth appears not only in Genesis and the Babylonian epic of Gilgamesh but also in the mythologies of China, India, Africa, Polynesia, and the Americas. All describe incessant rain followed by a flood and the appearance of a mythical bird that restores vegetation and regenerates life. In several of the North American Indian versions, all living things except for a couple of individuals drown in a great deluge that destroys the land. The survivors take refuge on a raft or an oak log and seek a mountaintop. There is a haunting similarity in all these stories of evil wiped out and of a chosen few starting a new world of goodness and optimism on an isolated mountaintop. Everywhere in the world the flood is associated with transformation.

Noah and the Ark

Noah, like his counterparts the Chaldean Tezpi and the Indian Utnapish-tim, saves a microcosm of the world in his ark when the rest is destroyed by a great deluge. His name may derive from Nuah, an earlier Babylonian moon goddess who sent destruction by flood but offered salvation to her chosen children in the form of a crescent-shaped boat, or ark. The word *ark* is a cognate of the Hindu word *argha,* which means "crescent"—the moon boat of the Hindus that transports souls to a new incarnation. In the Old Testament the word for ark is *tebah,* which also designates the basket in which Moses was discovered floating down the Nile.

As recorded on the Eleventh Tablet of Creation, the Babylonian moon goddess Ishtar, like her predecessor Nuah, prophesied a flood that would devastate the earth. When her prophecy came to pass and she witnessed all the animals and people being destroyed, she was filled with sorrow:

> *As I prophesied in the presence of the gods evil, to evil were devoted all my people and I prophesied*
> *I the mother have begotten my people and like the young of the fishes they fill the sea*
> *The gods concerning the spirits were weeping with me*
> *The gods seated in lamentation covered with their lips for the coming evil*
>   *Six days and nights passed*
> *The wind, the deluge, storm overwhelmed.*
> *On the seventh day in its course, was calmed the storm and all the deluge.*

Although the message of these events is extremely archetypal and symbolic, the flood myth does not seem to be purely a psychological event. Assyrian tablets from the library of Ashurbanipal testify to the arrival of survivors of a great flood in a large ship built by a king-priest. There is also archaeological evidence of an actual deluge. Excavations at the Chaldean city of Ur have revealed the remains of a civilization buried under a ten-foot layer of silt containing no life forms. In both the Persian Gulf and the Gulf of Mexico, oil rigs dig through rich alluvial clay beneath which are remnants of antedeluvian life. Similar discoveries have been found in Asia, including evidence of a tragic event in 2297 B.C., after which the River Hwang became known as China's Sorrow. All of this leads us to believe that the flood myth may in fact reflect one of the greatest natural disasters of all time.

Say, you are in the country; in some high land of lakes. Take almost any path you please, and ten to one it carries you down in a dale and leaves you there by a pool in the stream. There is magic in it. Let the most absent-minded of men be plunged in his deepest reveries—stand that man on his legs, set his feet a-going, and he will infallibly lead you to water, if water there be in all that region. . . . Yes, as every one knows, meditation and water are wedded forever.

HERMAN MELVILLE, *Moby Dick*

Sacred Wells and Springs

Fountains of Youth and Immortality

The belief in the sacredness of life-giving water at the sources of rivers, springs, and wells is an ancient one. There was a time when a story or a legend surrounded each well or spring. Each was magical, perceived as a dwelling place for beings who acted as intermediaries between gods and mortals. Sometimes they were associated with saints who had appropriated their waters for performing miracles, and at other times with evil spirits, ghosts, or monsters who threatened the well-being of people unless they were somehow appeased. Contact with these waters either healed or harmed people. As a result, the wells themselves came to be regarded as oracles and sacred shrines. "Where a spring rises or a water flows," declared the Roman philosopher Seneca, "there ought we to build altars and offer sacrifices." And they did.

Well worship became part of everyday reality in diverse regions of the world—not only in Eastern countries with dry climates, such as India, where water was valued more than gold, but in cool, lush Northern countries as well. What began as a pagan tradition was later adopted by Christians. Even today we hear of living water that heals the sick, rejuvenates the old, restores sight, and reassembles dismembered bodies.

Every culture's folklore boasts its own fountain of youth and immortality or well of knowledge. In the early Christian liturgy, for example, the

Paul Signac, Les Femmes au puits, 1892, oil on canvas, 76¾ × 51½ in. (195 × 131 cm). Musée d'Orsay, Paris

Holy Sepulcher is described as the fountain of life and resurrection. The *zhivaya voda* of Slavic lore is sacred water that has the power to bring the dead back to life. The Aztec god Quetzalcoatl drinks from the Water of Immortality when he sails on his raft of snakes toward the land of the sun.

In 1513 the Spanish conquistador Ponce de León set out on an expedition to Florida, determined to find the fountain of youth. Many of the springs looked promising, but eventually he gave up. The Maidu and Wintun Indians of California believed that in the time before death entered the world, people could regain their youth by diving into the water of life. This life-giving attribute of water spawned magic rituals aimed at restoring virility in men and bringing the dead back to life. It became a cult.

According to the second-century Greek rhetorician Lucian, the mysterious Seres people, whose land was somewhere between Scythia and India, lived until the age of three hundred years. He wrote, "Some attribute this longevity to the air, others to the soil, others again to the diet. In fact, it is said that the whole race drinks nothing but water." The astonishment of Westerners at the water-drinking Chinese was rivaled only by the astonishment of the Chinese at the wine-drinking Westerners.

Ed. Tapissier, The Fountain of Youth, *Salon de Paris, 1913*

*European baths, a
copper etching by
Virgil Solis, tenth
century.*

Early Chinese writings are full of respect for water's rejuvenative powers. Wang Chia of the Chin Dynasty noted that "the bubbling fountain of
Pon Lai gives a thousand lives to those who drink it." Likewise, the springs
of Mount Lao Shan had the reputation of being the elixir of life, and even
the emperors of the Chin and Han dynasties made pilgrimages to them.

There were also many legends about fountains of love and of hate. The
gardens of Venus, for example, had two fountains: one of sweet waters, the
other of bitter. When Venus (Aphrodite) became jealous of Psyche's beauty,
she sent her son Cupid (Eros) to destroy her. Cupid filled two amber vases,
one from each fountain, and went to see Psyche. He found her sleeping and
poured a drop of the bitter waters on her lips as his mother had instructed.
Psyche stirred and he saw her loveliness. He fell so deeply in love with her
beauty that he kissed the bitterness off her lips and instead poured the
sweet waters of joy on his beloved.

The Healing Waters

The cult of the wells and springs was often connected with a life-giving goddess and imagined to be the gates to a mystical reality. The association of streams with the eyes, breasts, and mouth of the goddess emphasized her role as a benevolent dispenser. Her task was to ensure life, health, and abundance from the divine life source.

Water is often allegorically associated with the primal egg, a frequent motif in the decorated pottery of the ancient world. Rain-bearing and milk-giving motifs are interwoven, and anthropomorphic vases and jugs representing the Great Goddess, commonplace in her shrines, are used in rituals. Also depicted in the form of a bird, fish, or snake, she suggests the life-giving force of water. The snake itself most likely represents the S-shaped meandering of water and was an indispensable and ubiquitous symbol in prehistoric cultures.

The Greeks enshrined their sacred springs by erecting artificial basins at their sources and placing icons of their special deities nearby. Roman, Celtic, and Baltic myths are replete with goddesses and nymphs connected to certain rivers, springs, and wells. Rivers, for example, were often named after goddesses. The Boyne and Shannon rivers in Ireland allegedly owe their names to the goddesses Boann and Sinann. The River Dee, also called Dyfrdwy, which means "water of divinity," was worshiped by the Celts as the goddess Aerfon. The Seine in France was named after the healing goddess Sequana of the Gauls. Hundreds of wooden figures discovered in a Gallo-Roman sanctuary at the source of the Seine in the 1960s suggest a belief in the healing powers of the waters emanating from the river's source.

As we observed before, the Roman spring Egeria was linked with a fountain nymph who fell in love with Numa Pompilius, the second king of Rome. The lovers had nocturnal trysts in a sacred grotto during which Egeria not only made love with the king but inspired him to establish his codex of laws. After Numa's death, the nymph wept so copiously that she was transformed into a fountain. Lord Byron exalted her in canto 4 of *Childe Harold:*

> *Here didst thou dwell, in this enchanted cover,*
> *Egeria! all thy heavenly bosom beating*
> *For the footsteps of the lover;*
> *The purple midnight veiled that mystic meeting*
> *With her most starry canopy.*

Other life-giving goddesses, such as the Baltic Laima and the Irish Brigit, are also associated with sources of wells and springs. There is still a venerated shrine to St. Brigit in the county Louth at Faughart, an area full of megalithic tombs, where people make annual pilgrimages. On the first day of spring all her devotees visit the wells and perform the rites. First, they wash their hands and feet; then, tearing a small rag from their clothes, they affix it to a tree overhanging the well. This rag or ribbon is considered to be the symbol of the suppliant's spiritual or bodily ailments. Therefore it acts not merely as a votive offering but also as a riddance.

The Russian saint Praskeva Pyatnitsa was a patroness of healing springs where the paralyzed, the blind, and the deaf came to make offerings of flax, wool, and sheep, which served the same purpose as the rags.

Lourdes in France, designated as a site of miracles, is also a place of pilgrimage for the afflicted. The first healing at Lourdes was claimed in the mid-nineteenth century by Louis Bouriette, a stonebreaker who had lost his sight. When Bouriette applied mud from the spring in Lourdes's grotto of Massabielle to his eyes, he regained full vision. Two-year-old Justin Bouhourts was suffering from severe convulsions and from atrophy of the lower half of his body. In an act of desperation, his mother rushed him to the grotto and dipped him in the water. Witnesses claimed that he was healed instantly.

The cures never seemed to end and were mostly inexplicable. Tumors the size of a human head disappeared after steady use of Lourdes spring water. Paralysis greatly improved within a matter of days. Several people were cured between one breath and the next. Others recovered more slowly but just as mysteriously.

The medical establishment, as disinclined to favor the competition of heaven as that of any quack, examined each case meticulously and submitted a report to the Church. Even though the bishop would only consider

Pamukkale Hot Springs, Turkey.

North of the Taurus Mountains lies Pamukkale, the ancient sacred city of Hierapolis, one of the most enchanting sights in Turkey. Its dazzling white cliffs, almost 400 feet high, rise in a snowy cascade of limestone deposits and shallow ponds, creating an unworldly spectacle. The healing waters were famous in Roman times, and people still come from everywhere to bathe in the warm, soporific springs and benefit from their restorative properties. At the bottom of an ancient sacred pool one can still see classical columns, capitals, and other fragments of antiquity.

validating the instantaneous cures, tens of thousands of people began making pilgrimages to Lourdes seeking new health and life.

Emperor Napoleon's son, nicknamed Loulou, was once suffering from a dangerously high temperature. His mother, Empress Eugénie, ordered the destruction of the barricades that had been blocking the grotto, and the child was cured by the waters of the Massabielle grotto. His recovery was considered a near-miracle, at least in the political sense, motivating the Church finally to take the visions and healings at Massabielle into serious consideration.

When I was a young girl in Istanbul, we often traveled to the tomb of Kuyu Baba, a Sufi saint, who was reputed to grant just about anything. We would tie rags next to hundreds of others that were dancing in the wind around his tomb, which was by a spring, and then would make wishes, offering him a sacrifice if our wish was granted. Once a rooster gave its life because I passed my exams. After that, I stopped going to the saint.

According to a written account from the Dungiven parish in Ireland, people would proceed to a large river rock that had footprints imprinted in it. They walked around the rock, bowed, and prayed. If there were cupmarks, or miniature wells, in the rock, they would drink the water collected in them, because they believed in the water's miraculous healing powers.

In the Middle Ages the Marienkirche in Rostock, Germany, had a miraculous Madonna that attracted throngs of pilgrims. It was an ingenious sculpture. Her hollowed head was filled with water and little fish. As they swam, the water was forced out of her eyes, and supplicants assumed she was weeping for their sins.

The Great Goddess and Sacred Springs

In prehistory and folk memories, wells and cupmarks became interchangeable, both being symbols of the centrally concentrated goddess life force. Early civilizations often attributed healing powers to the rainwater that collected in these hollows; paralytics and people with other afflictions drank this holy water, washed themselves with it, and rubbed it on their afflicted parts. Cupmarks found throughout Europe still retain some of their symbolic significance in the peasant subculture.

As early as Paleolithic and Neolithic times, caves were the sites of sanctuaries. Many of these cave sanctuaries contained lakes, subterranean rivers, or hot springs. For example, a stream flows from the mouth of the caves at the Magdalenian sites of Montespan and Tuc d'Auboubert in southern France.

Ishtar, the Babylonian moon goddess, was connected with springs and dew, symbols of fertility. In a land where sun is the enemy, this is significant. Her temples were often in natural grottoes whose springs represented the source of life, or at oases in the desert. Like Ishtar, the moon goddesses of other cultures were also guardians of wells, rivers, and springs. Their shrines were usually in groves, or in grottoes where water trickled directly out of a rock. Ceremonies of water drawing and pouring were constantly performed for these goddesses.

During the Celtic era, in Niederbronn, Alsace, Diana was worshiped as the goddess of sacred wells, which were considered sources of fertility. Even now, women carry water from the mineral springs to the nearby mountains, where they pour it over stones, drawing circular patterns while making wishes to become pregnant. In Aargau, Germany, women believed that they would conceive if they bathed in the spring of Verena, a Christian saint of the Alemanni, who replaced Diana.

In many African tribes it was customary for women taking part in rainmaking ceremonies to visit the springs and clean them out, then draw fresh water and throw it over their naked bodies, purifying themselves.

Some tribes, such as the Baganda of central Africa, believed that a woman who was menstruating should not have any contact with wells; otherwise, the wells would dry up and the woman herself would become ill and die. On the Greek island of Kalymnos, a woman during her cycle is not allowed to draw water from a well, cross a stream, or swim in the sea. The islanders also believe that her presence in a boat raises storms; this may be the original source of the belief that a woman aboard ship is bad luck. The reason for secluding women during menstruation is supposedly to neutralize the dangers emanating from them at such times.

Prophecy

There, where on Sundays I go alone
To the old, old well with the milk-white stone
Where by the fence, in a nook forgot,
Rises a Spring in the daisied grass,
That makes whoso drinks of it love—alas!
But my heart's best beloved, he drinks it not.
*   Romanian folk song*

Wells and springs have mostly been places of solace, inhabited by gentle spirits blessed with gifts of prophecy. As such, they became places of pilgrimage and worship, secular temples adorned with sacred rocks and healing plants. Even after Judeo-Christian cultures prohibited such pagan indulgences, people still continued their pilgrimages to the sacred wells. And, in order to underplay their importance, they began referring to them as "wishing wells."

Each wishing well had its own special powers and attributes, and was endowed with a touch of melancholy. They were ancient sites of ritual, often located in the heart of a shrine or a parish. They also marked the boundaries of tribal territories.

By offering a needle or a coin to the wishing well, it was possible to get answers to nagging questions. Villagers in some parts of Cornwall, England, for example, visited St. Madran's well every first Sunday in May. After a sermon they threw pins into the well to consult the well spirit about personal issues like health, money, and affairs of the heart. The responses had a language of their own. If two pins sank together, it was an indication of marriage. If they floated flat, it was a premonition of illness.

Not all deities who occupied the rivers and wells were benevolent, however; some were downright nasty. For example, a well near the River Ribble at Clitheroe, in northern England, is said to be inhabited by Peg O'Nell, who has long been blamed for everything that has ever gone wrong in people's lives. Every year she claimed a victim, and it became customary to drown a bird or another animal in order to appease her.

There are legends about some springs and wells that had the power to cure not only spiritual and corporeal afflictions but also material ones. King Midas of Phrygia wished that everything he touched would turn to gold. He was supremely happy when his wish came true until mealtime, when everything he put in his mouth became metal. In desperation he consulted Bacchus, who advised him to plunge his head into the bubbling spring near Sardis. Midas obeyed, and the golden virtue departed from the human body into the spring.

In pagan times wells were not only the home of the gods but also the social center of the community. Everyone met at the well. Later, Christian missionaries preached by the wells and baptized converts there.

Well-Dressing

In Derbyshire Dales, England, there is a fascinating custom called "well-dressing." People collect thousands of flower petals and press them into a large clay base to form a beautiful sacred tableau that is then hung over a well and is blessed by holy men of all denominations. This floral thanksgiving for water, unique to the area, originated during pre-Christian days, when life-giving springs were worshiped as gods; it dates back to the ancient Roman festival of Fontinalia, celebrated on October 13 in honor of Fons, the god of fountains and wells. During Fontinalia, garlands were thrown into springs and placed around the tops of wells.

Water Witching, or Dowsing

The mysterious art of water witching, or dowsing, is considered a legitimate and common method for locating wells. A dowser is someone who seeks out underground water and determines where to sink wells by means of a pendulum or a divining rod. Dowsers claim to get a tingling sensation in their hands as they approach water, suggesting a force field similar to an electrical current. At the same time the rod vibrates and dips toward the ground, pointing to the water source.

Most dowsers, who are also called water witches, can not only find the water but also know how deep the well should go and how much water it will supply. Among the Cornish, there is a widespread belief that dowsers have a special, almost telepathic, connection to the spirits inhabiting underground wells.

Several cases have been reported in which a dowser has actually claimed to have seen the subterranean water. In *The Divining Rod,* Sir William Barrett cites the case history of a dowser named Miss Miles who located a lost underground cistern and was able to describe its appearance in detail. Some dowsers can locate wells from far away simply by using their divining rod or pendulum over a photograph or a map of a particular terrain. They have also been known to ask questions of the divining rod or the pendulum about other issues and to receive answers.

Water, it seems, has a highly active electromagnetic field around it. Apparently, long-term exposure to the radiation of water can have effects similar to radioactivity. Dowsers believe that sleeping above an underground stream causes illness and discomfort and recommend that people change their sleeping places accordingly.

The well-known French dowser Barthélemy Bleton felt sick every time he sat on a certain spot. Excavations at this spot revealed an underground cistern powerful enough to drive a mill wheel. Capt. Robert Boothby, a British dowser, asserted that underground streams cross prehistoric sites and that burial mounds have streams running below them. Likewise, Reginald Smith of the British Museum points out that there is a spot in the

center of every prehistoric site from which several streams project. He calls them "blind springs."

Guy Underwood, who studied prehistoric sites in England with a divining rod, discovered two kinds of magnetic forces, one at least twice as wide as the other. He called the narrower force "track lines" and the more powerful one "aquastats." They often consisted of two sets of parallel lines not unlike railway tracks. Track lines were followed by animals during their regular prowling. Underwood also discovered that many of the old roads were aligned along these tracks and that, instead of running in straight lines, they meandered like the tracks of a drunkard, or moved in a series of loops and S-bends. Sometimes the track lines formed whirlpools, which seemed especially significant in terms of locating ancient sacred sites. The great avenues of stone at Carnac, Brittany, for example, were built over parallel underground streams. But why did that make the site sacred? And how did the ancients use this force? We do not have the answers.

Underwood unveiled a principle of nature not yet identified by science. He described it in his posthumous work, *The Pattern of the Past* (1969): "The philosophers and priests of the old religions seem to have believed that—particularly when manifested by spiral forms—it [the earth force] was involved with . . . the generative powers of Nature; that it was part of the mechanism by which what we call Life comes into being; and to have been the 'Great arranger'—that balancing principle which keeps all Nature in equilibrium, and for which biologists still seek. Plato gave this force the name of 'Demiurge.'"

There are several schools of thought about why a divining rod reacts to concealed underground water. The most common is that water emits radiation and some humans have the ability to detect it. Believers contend that our ancestors needed this ability to survive droughts and that it has been dormant through our various stages of evolution. This does not, of course, explain why some people have the ability to dowse and others do not. The second explanation is that the dowser emits radiation that bounces back like radar. And the third is that dowsing depends on a subconscious mind able to answer questions that the conscious mind cannot. But there is still no scientific explanation for water witching. However inexplicable it may be, it is often a successful way of locating underground water and is resorted to even by the establishment when all else fails.

The Legends of Springs

In the center of Mecca is a spring called Zamzam. According to a Moslem legend, Abraham's son Ishmael and Ishmael's mother, Hagar, ran out of their water supply while crossing the desert. Hagar climbed several mountains in search of water, while Ishmael sifted sand through his fingers. Suddenly a spring bubbled out of the sand. Since then, when Moslems make their holy pilgrimage, part of their ritual is to drink the water from the Zamzam spring.

The red stain of iron deposits found in the water of some wells was often assumed to be blood. A Welsh legend involves a maiden named Winifred who was courted by a prince named Cracodus, who, on finding his love spurned, cut off her head. Suddenly the earth opened and swallowed up Cracodus. And from the place where Winifred's head had fallen burst a spring, spreading a crimson stain. St. Bueno picked up the head and reunited it with the body. The spring became famous for its cures.

King Vakhtang of Iberia, an ancient region south of the Caucasus, shot a deer while he was hunting. The wounded animal desperately leaped into a warm sulfur spring and magically darted away. The king was so impressed that he built his capital around the springs in Tbilisi, Georgia, which means "warm springs." This legend resembles the one about Blaudad, the king/shepherd of Britain: when he communicated leprosy to his flock, the afflicted animals leaped into the nearby hot springs and emerged cured. Blaudad followed their example with the same results. This spring came to be known as Aquae Sulis in Roman times and later as Bath—one of the most incredible watering holes in the world.

During the Romantic period wells and fountains held a great fascination. In their stone, people sometimes engraved verses, as Sir Walter Scott records:

> *Where shall she turn?—behold her mark*
>   *A little fountain cell,*
> *Where water, clear as diamond spark,*
>   *In a stone basin fell.*
> *Above, some half-worn letters say,*
> *DRINK-WEARY-PILGRIM-DRINK-AND-PRAY*
> *FOR-THE-KIND-SOUL-OF-SYBIL-GREY*
> *WHO-BUILT-THIS-CROSS-AND-WELL.*
>   SIR WALTER SCOTT, *Marmion*

What must be acknowledged is the mysterious way the wells have inspired the most potent factor in any healing—faith. They appeal to those who believe in magic, love potions, the evil eye, and other superstitious evasions of personal responsibility. The healing pool of Bethesda in Jerusalem, the Moon Washing Spring in Japan, and the Great Saliva Lake of the Tang Dynasty in China are all legendary springs that are believed to possess extraordinary healing powers. During the Middle Ages in Europe, springs were worshiped as the source of miraculous cures. Attempts during the Reformation to change this custom were in vain, for little else provided hope for the afflicted.

As the Romans conquered their way through Europe, they spread not only the worship of deities, but also their water rituals. Pagan wells evolved into holy wells. Enshrined, eventually they became the baths—the nucleus of an entire culture and proven health centers for centuries.

Allegorical outline of the history of Rogaška Slatina Springs, Rogaška Slatina Hot Springs, Czechoslovakia.

TAKING
THE
WATERS

Baths

Ritualistic Communion with Water

The cult of the bath reflects the attitudes that the bathers held toward their bodies, sin, nudity, relaxation, and religion. While most societies developed different ways of creating physical contact with water, incorporating the philosophy and temperament of their people and their environment, they always seemed to have the same elements in common—spiritual, hygienic, therapeutic, and social. A few societies, however, considered bathing a disagreeable chore, finding it easier to stink than to take a plunge.

Cleaning wounds in fresh streams was something that humans learned from animals. Families in primitive cultures bathed together, sharing the same watering place. Since they did not yet possess the means of heating water, they took cold baths.

Jean-Léon Gérôme, The Bath, ca. 1880–85, oil on canvas, 29 x 23½ in. (73.7 x 59.7 cm). The Fine Arts Museums of San Francisco, Mildred Anna Williams Collection

May Baths

To ritualize the beginning of summer, both the Germanic and Celtic tribes celebrated May Day, which was not a calendar day but an occasion that evolved over thousands of years of observing the return of flowers and mi-

The Bath, *n.d.,*
miniature from the
Roman du bon roi
Alexandre.

gratory birds, and the birth of domestic animals. When the snow and ice began to melt and lilacs rose out of the dead land and springs gushed forth again, people's excitement and their gratitude toward nature were expressed in the May Bath, which simply entailed bathing in a spring or, symbolically, in a tub filled with May herbs.

A similar celebration, Midsummer's Day, also known as St. John the Baptist's Day, was held in June. It was a time for washing away worries and sorrows, a time for new beginnings, hopes, and dreams. In Sweden, on St. John's Eve people visited certain holy springs considered to be endowed with great medicinal powers in the hopes of healing their various infirmities. "One bath on St. John's Day equals nine baths at other times" read the entrance sign at Bad Württemberg. Because of this belief, people flocked to the water towns to celebrate St. John's Day and to get rid of their afflictions before beginning a new cycle in their lives.

Although condemned by the Church, May Day and similar rituals continued well into the Middle Ages. Medieval art often portrayed naked men and women bathing communally and joyously partaking of food and drink. The Church perceived this practice as an obsession, a remnant of pagan consciousness influenced by the heathen Walpurgis Night rituals, but its efforts to suppress May Day activities were in vain. In 1488, Margrave Christof of Baden-Baden decreed: "On the Eve of May, every person excepting children shall go on that very evening to the free baths."

Because of its ritualistic significance, for a long time people bathed only in the season of spring. But when the therapeutic aspects of bathing became better understood and water became more portable, bathing became a yearlong activity, and various forms of bathhouses sprang up everywhere.

The Major Bathing Traditions

Edmond Paulin,
Restitution of
Diocletian Bath, *ca.*
1880, engraving.
Bibliothèque de
l'Ecole Nationale Su-
périeure des Beaux-
Arts, Paris

The role that bathing plays within a culture reveals the culture's attitude toward hu-
man relaxation. It is a measure of how far individual well-being is regarded as an
indispensable part of community life.

SIEGFRIED GIEDION, *Mechanization Takes Command*

The Greeks favored cleanliness, but bathing for them was not an indulgence. They bathed after a strenuous physical workout, and prior to intellectual discussion, at the gymnasiums of Plato's time, the centers for
refining philosophical discourse.

At no time before or since has bathing taken on such magnificent and
ritualized proportions as during the Roman Empire. The Roman poet Juve-
nal coined the phrase *mens sana in corpore sano* (a sound mind in a sound
body), and the Romans took the maxim to heart, embracing it with true
conviction. They believed in equilibrium for wholeness and created environments for maintaining that equilibrium. Roman *thermae,* or baths, combined physical fitness, social interaction, and entertainment. They were
institutions that reflected a holistic conception of health. Their sophisticated and elaborate bathing practices led to the creation of enormous
shrines and architectural edifices like the Diocletian and Caracalla baths,
which were the natural consequence of an essentially hedonistic approach
to life. Without strong counteracting morals and values, the baths eventually facilitated excessive sensuality, and public bathing went the way of
the Pax Romana.

The Finns developed a spiritual as well as social attitude toward the sauna. It was not simply a place to sweat and douse oneself with water but also a place of healing. Babies were born in saunas and the dead were laid out in them before funerals. To exorcise the devil, the possessed were taken into the sauna and beaten with a *vihta*—a whisk made of small birch branches—until the evil spirits departed.

Moslems were convinced that relaxed bathing led to enlightenment and were drawn to bathing's meditative and social aspects. The bath, or *hamam,* became the Islamic water temple, where rejuvenation was a spiritual issue—repose and solitude mingled with sensous contemplation.

During its golden era, Baghdad boasted thirty thousand bathhouses. The wealth that made this luxury possible came not from gold but from the muddy waters of Mesopotamia. Baths were so important to the Arabs that when they conquered Alexandria, they allegedly burned seven hundred thousand books in the library so as to keep up the fires in the four thousand public hamams.

In Japan, bathing was practiced as a means of maintaining balance with the forces of nature. A great deal of time was spent in outdoor baths meditating on the harmony of the opposites, the Tao of nature.

Grecian Baths

The Greeks were among the first to create public baths. Delphi itself, at the foot of Mount Parnassus, was a vast watering place. Bathing was a necessary antidote to the sweaty labors of the gymnasium and to the dust and blood of the battlefield. An essential part of the Greek gymnasium, the edu-

Baths of ancient Rome.

cational core of the society, was the therapeutic use of water. The Greeks followed a rigorous routine that included bathing in a circular pool between a strenuous physical workout in the palaestra (gym, wrestling ring) and a philosophical discussion in the exedrae (discussion halls). Hippocrates, the father of Western medicine, used hydrotherapy extensively to help combat disease. Because of the calming effects of warm water, bathing was also an early treatment for the mentally disturbed. But the main purpose of the baths was to provide water to the masses and encourage cleanliness.

Initially, the Greeks considered immersion in a hot bath self-indulgent and effete, but by the fifth century B.C., they were building efficient bathhouses for men and women both. Long before, Homer had made frequent references to bathing, as in this passage from the *Iliad:* "when the inward heart had been cooled to refreshment they stepped into the bathtubs smooth-polished, and bathed there, and after they had bathed and anointed themselves with olive oil they sat down to dine."

Soap, made from a mixture of ashes and goat fat, was widely utilized. To revitalize their bodies, the Greeks also used sponges, oils, rinses, and a curved metal instrument for scraping oneself called a strigil, which was supposed to collect whatever was eliminated by the pores.

Roman Baths

The Romans deserve the credit for combining the spiritual, social, and therapeutic values of bathing and exalting it to an art. In the warm Roman climate, *thermae* were a welcome part of the day; going to the baths became a social pleasure. Baths were the focus of communal life, offering a place for relaxation, social gathering, and worship.

Historians explain the growth of public bathing as a function of mounting prosperity in the Roman Empire. By the third century B.C. wealthy Romans had bathing chambers in their town houses and country villas, but bathing was still a private act and a great deal of modesty was attached to it. Gradually, however, the Roman obsession for cleanliness led to public bathing. In 33 B.C. the Roman soldier and statesman Agrippa built the Julia aqueduct at Rome and introduced free public bathhouses that included hot baths, tepid baths, cold baths, and massage rooms. The bathhouses were separated into two parts, the *balneae,* or communal part, and the *balneum,* or private bath.

The way water was supplied to the city of Rome is one of the marvels of ancient times. In 312 B.C., Appius Claudius Caecus built the first aqueduct on the Appian Way; it was eleven miles long and partly subterranean. This caused such a sensation that an aqueduct craze spread throughout the country. The ducts bringing water to Rome from the surrounding hills soon totaled 381 miles in length. Suddenly there was enough water not only for utilitarian purposes but for pleasure as well.

Since iron piping was unknown at the time, lead was the primary material available to carry water under pressure. In a startling preview of our own environmental problems with toxic materials such as asbestos and aluminum, the lead eventually caused poisoning and sterility among the population. Only much later was the source of the trouble traced back to the lead pipes of the aqueducts and plumbing.

The Romans had other problems that seem alarmingly similar to our own. The water supply to the cities, for example, was distributed from terminal reservoirs. Frontinus, water commissioner of Rome during the first century under Emperor Nerva, left a very human document in which he revealed his frustration about keeping the public supply flowing:

> *The cause for this is the fraud of the water-men whom we have detected diverting water from the public conduits for private use; but a large number of proprietors of land also, whose fields border on the aqueducts, tap the conduits; whence it comes that the public water courses are brought to a standstill by private citizens, yea, for the water of their gardens.*
>
> *Frontinus & the Water Supply of Rome* (100 A.D.)

Each day, 750 million liters of water flowed through 13 aqueducts, providing immense supplies of water for Rome's 1,352 public fountains, 11 imperial *thermae,* and 926 public baths. Each citizen consumed about 300 gallons of water a day—the average water consumption for a family of four in our time. (In 1991, for example, when severe drought threatened California, citizens of Marin County were restricted to just 50 gallons per person, per day.)

The inclination of the rulers to satisfy their subjects' desires fostered the development of bathing establishments. Caesars seeking popularity

Women exercising, ca. A.D. 350, mosaic from a Roman villa, Piazza Armerina, Sicily.

built *thermae* for their people and soon philanthropists followed, building their own elaborate baths as a sort of public relations gesture. Thus the bathhouse evolved from a simple wood-enclosed, single-function unit, small and austere, into a complex, luxurious, spacious, multifunctional establishment. The Romans' respect for water was manifested in the construction of monumental *thermae* and sculptural fountains—water shrines where physical, cultural, and intellectual pursuits complemented one another. According to legend, upon seeing the magnificent fountains of Rome, Emperor Nero exclaimed, "Sanitas per aquas" (health through water). The word *spa* may be an acronym of this famous phrase.

Some of the Roman bathhouses were spectacular achievements even by modern-day standards, combining many of the elements that make life attractive. The ruins of the Diocletian and Caracalla baths, for example, are still impressive. Diocletian's bathhouse covered an area of over 13 hectares—about 32.5 acres—and could accommodate as many as 6,000 people. The floors were mosaic; the walls were covered with Egyptian marble, ornamental stone and glass, and exquisite frescoes. It contained a library, galleries, gymnasiums, and offered an assortment of entertainment. Its stadium was in a great covered space with marble seats at each end, which accommodated approximately 1,600 people. The entire building was bordered by a portico that opened up to the exedrae, the spacious halls used by poets and philosophers.

The Caracalla baths had a temple at each end—one dedicated to Apollo and the other to Aesculapius, the deities responsible for nurturing mind and body respectively. Outside, the gardens of philosophers featured grottoes and nymphaea watered by fountains and springs, shaded porticos displaying masterpieces of sculpture, an odeum for music, and tree-lined promenades for strolling. The impressive group of buildings constituting the *thermae* were surrounded by an esplanade cooled by shade and dancing fountains.

The Romans developed an efficient form of central heating for the baths, the hypocaust—a room with a cavity beneath the floor, where hot air circulated. Adjacent to the room was a charcoal-fueled flue that commonly had a large copper boiler set above it so as to provide a constant supply of hot water. Vertical flues with openings through the roof were set into the walls of the hypocaust. These flues created a draft that drew hot air into the underfloor chamber.

In its simplest form, a bathhouse would consist of an *apodyterium* (dressing room), a *frigidarium* (cold bath), a *tepidarium* (tepid bath), a *caldarium* (hot bath), and possibly a palaestra (exercise court). More sophisticated establishments, such as Aquae Aureliae (Baden-Baden) and Aquae Sulis (Bath) also had a *laconium* (a room of intense dry heat), not unlike the Finnish sauna.

Bathing was a lively occasion, considered essential for one's well-being. Romans had learned a great deal about the sybaritic aspects of bathing from the Egyptians, who found it both soothing and sensual to bathe in ass's milk, crushed strawberries, or aromatic spices, the most popular being saffron and cinnamon, for which large fortunes were spent.

The intricate architectural layout of the *thermae* gave birth to an elaborate bathing ritual. While it varied from bathhouse to bathhouse, it is possible to re-create what was probably a fairly general routine. The baths opened to the public at 1:00 P.M., at which time an attendant would ring a bell signifying that the water was hot. After exercising, the bathers would first go to the *apodyterium* to undress and get a bathing sheet. They would then enter the *tepidarium* to acclimate their bodies to the heat before moving on to the *caldarium* to take a hot-water bath. They were now ready for the *laconium,* an extremely hot chamber, above a furnace, that made one sweat as much as possible. Afterward they would be oiled, massaged, and scraped with a strigil, and the treatment would end with a quick plunge in the *frigidarium,* which closed the pores and revitalized the bathers. The alternative was a cold swim in a *natatorium* (pool), which served essentially the same purpose. Now relaxed and refreshed, they could socialize and make use of the libraries and other facilities.

Thermae were social gathering places where friends met and talked, business meetings were held, and various entertainments were performed. Actors, jugglers, slaves, and beauticians scurried around, tending to the needs of their masters and clientele. Those who could afford slaves brought them to the baths so that the slaves could rub down, massage, and anoint their masters. There is a saying that Rome fell because too many people spent too much time in the public baths.

In the earlier days of the *thermae* the men and women had separate facilities, but it was not long before mixed bathing became acceptable. People who wanted privacy still had the option of bathing in the *balneum,* but most bathers chose to enjoy the pleasures of mixed company. Many went to the baths because they found bathing to be a stimulant for food and sex. Lurking behind the magnificent porticoes were vendors of food and drink, as well as procurers of both sexes. "Baths, wine, and women corrupt our bodies," declared one participant; "but these things make life itself." Eventually, bathhouses began to be referred to as *seminaria venetata* or centers of promiscuity, and the word *bagnio* became synonymous with brothel. Finally the authorities could no longer ignore the scandals. Sometime between A.D. 117 and 138, Hadrian issued a decree that separated the sexes in the *thermae*.

Hadrian himself often bathed in the public baths with everyone else. One day he saw an old soldier he had known busily rubbing himself against the warm bricks. When he asked the man why he was doing this, the man replied that he could not afford to have slaves. Immediately he was given money and slaves. The next day, when the emperor went to the baths, all the other old men were rubbing themselves against the bricks.

Imperial baths were not only palaces of Roman water but palaces of the Roman people. Despite the decadent social and moral aspects, the immense contribution of the baths to Roman social life cannot be ignored. They promoted not only cleanliness but also an admiration for sports and culture. The prevalence of the nude figure in both Greek and Roman sculpture, in terms of design and symmetry, indicates peoples who celebrated a healthy and beautiful body just as much as they honored a quick and agile mind. Daily regeneration was a social responsibility, with emphasis on relaxation and pleasure.

As the Romans conquered Europe, they took their water pleasures with them, building sybaritic bathhouses throughout their empire, appropriating the healing waters of the local folk, and using them for communal rejuvenation and recreation. When the average Roman warrior was not out plundering, he was soaking in the baths.

The early bathhouses in the provinces were mostly frequented by soldiers and other young people who indulged in juvenile enthusiasms and pushed social limits to the breaking point. When the empire moved to Constantinople in A.D. 330, the *thermae* and aqueducts at Rome fell into a state of disrepair. In 527 Justinian I, sovereign of the Byzantine Empire, forbade mixed bathing.

Jewish Baths

The ancient Jews also regarded regeneration as a basic social responsibility but reduced bathing to an almost ascetic activity, devoid of pleasure or relaxation. The bath for the ancient Jew was unifunctional, with cleanliness its only goal, although religious and social values underlay the various practices. Arising from a concept of purification and puritanical view of nudity, Jewish bathing practices were soon prescribed in the Mosaic code of law, which was essentially devised for nomadic tribes.

Contact with the Babylonians acquainted the Jews with more evolved Sumerian bathing practices. In 1055 B.C., during the period of urbanization of the ancient Jews, King David began construction of a great waterworks and baths that were completed under Solomon. Bathing was no longer simply for the sake of cleanliness but for spiritual purification, gaining its authority from the Talmudic reference, "A Jew may not live in a city where there is no public bath."

Besides routine and overall cleanliness, Mosaic law covered the washing of specific parts of the body at specific times, based on references in the Bible and the Talmud. Bathing was prescribed after every act of conjugal intercourse, after childbirth, and after menstruation. A Jew had to wash after touching a corpse and after traveling. The cleansing ritual was also incorporated into preparations for the holiest day of the Jewish calendar, Yom Kippur.

The *mikvah,* or community bath, arose perhaps because the virtues of cleanliness were bound together with spiritual considerations, forming both a practical and an ethical code of conduct for Jewish people. The dimensions of a *mikvah* were roughly twenty feet square, and all were built below ground level, suggesting that natural sources of water from either springs or wells were used. The *mikvah* in Friedberg, Germany, one of the oldest of its kind, was reached by descending seventy-seven steps. Unadorned, made of rough stone, practically constructed, the *mikvah* embodied the Jewish attitude toward bathing: the bath was functional, ascetic, ritualistic.

Bathing and Early Christianity

Early Christians viewed the public bathhouses that the Romans had spawned all over Europe, segregated or not, as an immoral and unnecessary

Dan May, Devil in the Baths, *1989, monoprint, 11⅞ x 15 in. (29.7 x 38.1 cm). Collection of William and Georgia May*

indulgence. Cleanliness was equated with the luxury, materialism, and excessive sensualism of Rome; this made dirt a badge of holiness, and not washing oneself a pious act of self-denial. Many abstained from bathing altogether, thus mortifying the flesh as a penance for sin, while others retreated to private baths.

The Christians disapproved of the perfumes and cosmetics sold at the Roman baths, viewing them as a sign of moral decay. They also condemned nudity in bathing, which had been a natural state for the Romans. Nude or clothed, a good Christian would not bathe with a Jew and would be reluctant to do so with an excommunicated person.

Fountain of Youth, illustration from Codex de Sphaera, Modena, fifteenth-century.

Miniature from the Roman de Girart de Nevers et de la belle Euriant(?), French, fifteenth century.

The Christian Church restricted cleanliness, especially for those who were young and healthy. St. Benedict considered an unwashed body a temple of piety. St. Agnes, the child martyr, supposedly did not wash her face for eight years after her visionary experience. Dirtiness became a sign of self-abnegation and humility among the ascetic cults, as well as among a few of the monastic orders.

By the fifth century the hygienic practices of the Romans and Greeks were all but forgotten in most of Europe. The bathhouses disintegrated from lack of use. A few European monasteries, however, managed to preserve the hydrological technology and cleanliness habits of the Roman Empire. The monastery in Canterbury, for example, utilized elaborate plumbing with devices to purify water and transport it to different parts of the cloister. The monks who deviated into worldly behavior were sometimes ordered to take cold baths so as to awaken their mind. Annual hot baths became a ritual, with the highest priest taking the first bath and novices the last. Ailing monks were given the privilege of taking more hot baths.

Bathing in the Middle Ages

In the early Middle Ages the bathhouses were replaced by round wooden tubs, often large enough to accommodate two or more people. The basic reason for the communal tub was the difficulty in providing hot water. In principle, the bather could lie down but in fact never did, in order to make room for others while the water was still hot.

The aristocracy and the clergy codified washing into a ritual for their guests—the custom known as *donner à laver,* where one offered a washing, generally before eating meals. A basin was brought to the table and the guests washed their face and hands. Often the water was scented, or petals from roses or other fragrant flowers were strewn in the basin, which was ornamented with precious metals and painted decoratively. One could also flirt with one's neighbor.

The returning Crusaders brought back fantastic tales of the delights of the Islamic hamam; despite the strictures of the Church, Europe was once again enticed by the joys of communal waters. The word *hamam* in Arabic means "spreader of warmth." The desire for hamams brought on an interesting collaboration: the steam from breadbaking ovens was used to heat the baths. The bakers' guild and the bathmen's guild got into some conflict over this issue.

New baths were built on the site of old Roman ones and became known as centers of healing, treating everything from broken bones and nervous exhaustion to diseases of the heart, lungs, and brain. The pleasure principle played an equally significant role. In fact, much of what passed for bathing was less for the sake of cleanliness than for wholesale immersion in curative treatments and/or sensual delights. Men and women once again shared the baths, which facilitated dangerous liaisons. Musicians played while bathers sang, danced, drank, ate out of floating trays, and made love. It was not uncommon that someone died in the baths after indulging in a night of wanton behavior. "I have seen that common people spent twenty-four hours on end in the bath on St. John's Day," cites an eleventh-century account. "They not only underwent their cure but also ate, drank, and slept in the bath." It was the beginning of another scandalous era.

In Augsburg, Germany, as well as in many other parts of Europe, bathhouses contained private cubicles. The result was a vast number of illegitimate children. This caused such an uproar that the cubicles were closed on orders from the bishop. The Church did not care much whether people were clean or not, but it cared very much about their legitimacy. Different sessions were now assigned to each of the sexes; a ringing of bells announced the appropriate time for each sex to bathe.

During the Middle Ages, Europe was more in a state of destruction than construction. The use of polluted water caused many epidemics such as cholera that swept the continent. Thought to be a cause of infection, the public baths were condemned in 1350, when bubonic plague was at its height. Most of them closed at that time; those that did not became brothels. Bathhouses in England and France came to be known as "stew houses." In 1538, in order to eliminate sexual promiscuity and the spread of syphilis, Francis I of France ordered all "stews" demolished. England's Henry VIII followed suit, banning mixed bathing in 1546.

Hamams

In Spain, while her neighbors were caught up in the virtues of dirt and asceticism, bathing reached its height of sophistication, pleasure, and relaxation. The Moors, like their Roman predecessors, built bathhouses wherever they went—Córdoba alone had three hundred public baths just before its capture by the Christians in 1236. They also built aqueducts in Spain during the ninth century, and the Roman aqueduct in Seville was repaired.

The magnificent Alhambra, in Granada, which was built by Yusuf I, king of Granada from 1333 to 1354, exemplifies the style and grace of the Moorish baths. In layout and sequence, it was extremely similar to the Roman *thermae*. Light came in through star-shaped openings in the ceiling, adding another dimension of beauty to the experience of bathing. The upper part of the Chamber of Repose formed a gallery that could accommodate only two to four people at a time, leading one to believe that the baths were exclusively for the use of the sovereign and his harem.

Although the poetic, spiritual, and secluded nature of the Islamic garden was in contrast to the social and ceremonial aspects of Roman culture, the Moslems essentially adapted the Roman *thermae*. Hamams served as retreats linking physical and spiritual purification and, like the *thermae*, they had a sequence of hot and cold rooms. "Turkey is 'à la mode' among the water villages," wrote Gustave Flaubert in a letter from Istanbul. "The ambience of the baths evokes more the Oriental hamam than the Roman baths." Many of the hamams in the Ottoman Empire were renovated By-

> *Bathing in a woman's* hamam *took several hours, sometimes an entire day. The English author Julia Pardoe describes it in* Beauties of the Bosphorus *(1830): "The heavy, dense, sulphurous vapour that filled the place almost suffocated me—the subdued laughter and whispered conversations of . . . mistresses murmuring along in an undercurrent of sound—the sight of nearly three hundred women, only partially dressed, and that in fine linen so perfectly saturated with vapour that it revealed the whole outline of the figure— the busy slaves passing and repassing, naked from the waist upwards, and with their arms folded upon their bosoms, balancing on their heads piles of fringed or embroidered napkins—groups of lovely girls, laughing, chatting, and refreshing themselves with sweetmeats, sherbet, and lemonade—parties of playful children, apparently quite indifferent to the dense atmosphere which made me struggle for breath . . . all combined to form a picture like the illusory semblance of a phantasmagoria, almost leaving me in doubt whether that on which I looked were indeed reality, or the mere creation of a distempered dream."*

zantine originals and, until recently, Roman aqueducts supplied them with water.

In Islamic culture, rejuvenation was a spiritual process requiring repose and solitude. Although the hamam retained the sequence of hot and cold rooms, it discarded the other elements (gymnasium, exedrae, and library)

Jean-Léon Gérôme, Terrace of the Seraglio, *1886, photogravure, 7 x 10 in. (17.8 x 25.4 cm). Collection of the author*

of the Roman baths. Athletic activity was replaced by massage; intellectual discourse, by music and contemplation. The hamam was a place of non-activity and withdrawal, where even a slightly energetic movement could disturb the psychospiritual climate. It was a place to go in order to get away from the asphyxia of city life and leave one's daily existence behind. The body, having been marvelously purged of toxicity, stayed in a memoryless disorientation for hours, sometimes even days.

The sexes were always kept separate in the hamam. A central source often heated the two adjoining baths, with the women's bath on one side, the men's on the other. Men's hamams provided a special place of collective masculinity devoid of aggression, the serenity of water bringing about a horizontal and silent fraternity without locker-room wit and loud voices. For women, until the twentieth century, going to the hamam was the most important social and religious activity. It was also the only time they could leave their homes or harems and have contact with their friends. Women turned the bathing ritual into an art form. Lady Mary Wortley Montagu, who visited Istanbul in the early eighteenth century, called them "women's club houses."

After hours of being steamed, scrubbed, and pumiced, the bathers passed through a vestibule and a series of warm rooms into the center, where they were massaged and anointed. Then they moved to an adjoining *tepidarium,* a resting room where the sensual pleasure of bathing culminated in sweet exhaustion and relaxation. Here they were rinsed, left to rest on mattresses, given coffee, and told the latest gossip.

Hamams are still very much part of the social matrix of Turkey and other Islamic countries. Even large European cities such as Paris and London enjoy the exotic flavor of their own hamams.

Men's hamam, Istanbul.

The Decline of Bathing

The sixteenth century saw Europe enter a "dirty" decline; cleanliness reached an all-time low that lasted until the nineteenth century. Isabella of Castile, for example, was proud of the fact that she had only two baths during her lifetime—at birth and before her wedding. As a substitute for bathing, people used perfumes and cosmetics. The only people who stayed clean during this period were the Jews, whose religious obligations required them to take frequent baths.

Public bathing in Europe was somewhat rejuvenated in therapeutic form in the eighteenth century by John Wesley, the founder of Methodism, who preached the Mosaic precept "cleanliness is next to godliness." Wesley believed that cold baths could easily cure more than fifty afflictions. The attitude toward communal bathing began to shift again when the more prominent bathhouses returned to the ancient belief in water as healer.

In the seventeenth and eighteenth centuries, vapor baths, a variation on the steam bath, became extremely popular in France. They were connected to barbershops, because barbers in those days were considered men of medicine and many used hydrotherapy treatments regularly. But throughout most of Europe, bathing and provisions for bathing remained virtually nonexistent. Even with the coming of the industrial revolution, bathing did not immediately benefit from the new technology. The absence of plumbing made domestic hygiene impossible. In England, rapid urbanization, bringing with it congestion and slums, contributed to the severity of the cholera epidemic of 1832 and of subsequent outbreaks. An estimated fifty thousand people died in the epidemic and, as a result, the British were motivated to become pioneers in plumbing. London rapidly went from a city of cesspools to an intricate system of sewers. Cleansing stations were built all over the city in order to provide the public with baths and showers. Moving the tub indoors and giving it a location of permanence was one of the major social and architectural breakthroughs in the history of the bath.

The Private Bathroom

Since the time when social bathing became taboo, private baths have run their own course in the evolutionary history of bathing. People's attitudes toward their bodies changed over time and, consequently, environments designed to clean, cure, and beautify went through endless variations.

As early as 1800 B.C. the Minoans were using terra-cotta tubs very similar to modern ones. King Minos's palace in Knossos had hot and cold water running through an adroit plumbing system of interlocking ceramic pipes. The Minoans took their private bathing seriously and possessed great knowledge of the workings of water; they were the only people of their time who favored immersion. In addition to bathtubs, they also used flush toilets. Similarly, excavations in Mohenjo-Daro, Pakistan,

and Tel el Amarna, Egypt, have revealed elaborate bathrooms with advanced plumbing and showers. Such innovations were more than a convenience. They were instrumental in helping to reduce disease among dense urban populations and were also used ritualistically by the spiritual community. The priests of Tel el Amarna, for example, washed themselves from head to foot twice a day.

Wealthy Egyptians, too, savored the luxury of private baths. They built shallow tubs with showerlike attachments and embellished their bathwater with body ointments and perfumes, turning bathing into a potentially calming, rejuvenating, sensuous, and liberating experience. They often followed this with a massage of special aromatic oils—essentially, they were practicing "aromatherapy."

Although the Greeks and Romans enjoyed communal bathing, the rich had their own private facilities as well. The Greeks stood upright in tubs as water poured out of gargoyled heads above, or handmaidens poured it over them.

By the sixteenth century, showers had entered the bath scene in Europe. "There is water to drink here and to bathe in; a covered bath, vaulted and rather dark, half as wide as my dining room in Montaigne," wrote Michel de Montaigne during the summer of 1581 while staying at La Villa in Italy. "There is also a certain dripping apparatus they call *la doccia* (the shower): this consists of pipes by which you receive hot water on various parts of the body, and especially on the head, the water coming down on you in steady streams and warming the part of your body that they are beating down on; and then the water is received in a wooden trough, like that of washerwomen, along which it flows away. There is another bath, vaulted in the same way, and dark, for the women; the whole thing coming from a spring from which one drinks."

During the eighteenth century, when vanity was a virtue, many European nobles had private baths but most did not shy away from holding

court in them, free from feelings of modesty and guilt, and from the desire for privacy. In fact, while sitting in their baths they often had their portraits painted or had musicians perform for them.

Prerevolutionary French aristocrats used perfume instead of soap, their teeth rotted because they never cleaned them, and their fingers smelled of stale food. "The nobility urinated against the walls of marble corridors of Versailles," wrote Raymond Chandler in *The Long Goodbye,* "and when you finally got several sets of underclothes off the lovely marquise, the first thing you noticed was that she needed a bath." Cleanliness was undesirable, and natural human smell was in vogue. After one of his campaigns, Napoleon wrote to Josephine: "Will be home in three weeks. Don't wash." This suggests that he was turned on by her pheromones, secretions that attract the opposite sex.

Nevertheless, French royalty built magnificent tubs in their palaces that would be dismantled and reconstructed during subsequent reigns. During the reign of Louis XIV, cast-iron pipe was laid in France to transport water to Versailles. Gilt tubs were installed for the king; later, Marie Antoinette preferred marble tubs covered with cushions and trimmed with exotic fabrics. At least one hundred bathrooms were installed at Versailles. Casanova's bath in Paris had room for two; it was portable and stood at his bedside. For convenience, Parisian water sellers carried bathtubs in their carts and delivered them complete with hot water. During the eighteenth century shoe-shaped tubs called *sabotières* became fashionable, the intention of the design being to preserve modesty. Benjamin Franklin was responsible for bringing this style of tub to America in the 1780s. The *sabotière* was imprinted in history when Jean-Paul Marat was assassinated in his by Charlotte Corday.

LEFT: *W. Heath,* A Nice Place in Hot Weather, *or* Sabotière, *colored engraving.*

RIGHT: *Woman in a tub.*

The interior design of the bathroom, as well as the furniture, went through a lot of variations. During the Victorian era, for example, bathrooms were considered another parlor in the house, a place to cultivate oneself intellectually. Bookshelves lined the walls. Photographs of the period often depict women sitting and reading in bathtubs trimmed with lace.

In the United States, ownership of a bathtub was a mark of distinction, beginning with the installation of the first tub in the White House in 1851—though it is said that there was some initial opposition to it. Shortly, a dozen or so tubs made of Carrara marble were imported from Italy and installed in the Capitol. "The bathrooms of the Capitol are well patronized," wrote a Washington correspondent a century ago. "Fifty members of the lower House take a bath everyday, so the bath superintendent tells me, and nearly every congressman has a bath now and then at the expense of Uncle Sam." One day a member of Congress was in the tub when he was informed that his vote was needed immediately. Holding a wet towel around him, he ran to the floor of the House and voted.

In mid-nineteenth-century America, the "Saturday night bath" became popular. Although the original intent for this bath was religious—to prepare oneself for the Sabbath—it gradually came to be considered a ne-

The bath, 1900.

cessity. People were urged to use hot water in their bathing practices, especially in colder climates. Cold-water bathing was condemned by *The Delineator* magazine as "harmful & dangerous." As bathing became more common, the demand for private and improved bathroom facilities increased. Around mid-century, water heaters were introduced in private homes, but they were such perilous devices that they did more harm than good. It was not until the end of the nineteenth century that the design of heaters and other bathroom devices was perfected.

In 1906 the Ritz Hotel in Paris revolutionalized travel when it put a bath in every bedroom, inciting other luxury hotels to follow suit. In 1909 oversize President William Taft installed an oversize tub in the White House. The cast-iron bath came on the scene in about 1880; porcelain enamel was introduced around 1910. In 1911, flat tubs replaced the ones with feet or claws. By 1920 the cast-iron single-shell bathtub was in full production, but the only available color at first was white, which made the American bathroom look extremely antiseptic and clinical—a clear statement about its being a no-nonsense place for hygienic purposes and not for pleasure. "Though we know of gold, crystal, Cellini-like bathrooms," observed *House & Garden* magazine, "we believe that simplicity is not only wiser but more sanitary." The modern bathroom stressed functionality, privacy, and efficiency but did not differentiate between the various bodily functions. For the first time, elimination and bathing were confined to one and the same place.

Private bathrooms were still not common in American homes, except in larger cities, until after World War I. The city of Aurora, Illinois, decreed that every citizen must bathe at least once a week or go to jail. (There are no records of arrests.) During the 1920s a group called the Cleanliness Institute waged a "cleanliness crusade." Little comic books containing a special song were distributed at schools. The lyrics encouraged a good washing:

> *Clean hands and hearts may hope*
> *To find the way to happiness*
> *By using lots of soap.*

Procter & Gamble liked the idea and used the song to advertise Ivory soap. The soap market began to boom. Major perfumers came out with bubble baths, bath oils, and salts, as well as soap.

By 1927, bathrooms began to show signs of cheering up, and lavender, green, and blue tubs and tiles became the rage. Showers with a single round spray replaced the rows of water-squirting heads. Suddenly it was possible to luxuriate in one's own bathroom. Women developed a desire for larger bathrooms; concern for beauty had begun to complement hygiene. Since time immemorial, baths of queens and female deities—the Queen of Sheba, Semiramis, Cleopatra, Psyche, Venus, and so on—had been a compelling subject for artists. The concept of the desirable woman had always included her penchant for luxury or excessive indulgence in creature comforts and sensual pleasures. In the twentieth century, advertisements featuring movie stars and beauty queens languishing in great tubs full of bubble bath have played upon this fixation, and in its most commercial

form, bathing has been utilized for the marketing of bath and beauty products. "Take a bath in the dark tonight, and let the water make love to your
skin," suggests a perfume company advertisement.

If bathtubs have most often been identified with women, showers have
projected more of a masculine aura. The adjectives associated with bathing
suggest slowing down—soothing, relaxing, healing—whereas the adjectives prompted by the shower are more exciting—energizing, revitalizing,
refreshing.

When radio and television became commercial media, soap companies
began sponsoring soap operas, targeting women viewers. Men, after all,
purchased only 13 percent of the bath products. Today, commercials often
show men taking showers, but never bathing in a tub unless it is a spoof on
the Wild, Wild West, while women are shown in tub and shower both.
There is a clear distinction between the two: a woman in the shower portrays the wholesome, athletic working girl, whereas a woman in a tub, surrounded by bubbles, her skin glistening, her coif dripping wet, represents
the seductive, exotic type, always erotically provocative.

Jacuzzis, or whirlpool baths, were introduced at a country fair in 1968
by Roy Jacuzzi as a therapeutic item, operating on the same principle as
hydrotherapy, or underwater massage. But the public soon discovered their
recreational qualities. In 1978 a hot-tub boom hit the West Coast and gradually spread to other parts of the country. Partly because of the hot tub,
Marin County, California, gained the reputation of being a hotbed of
hedonism, as its inhabitants were depicted cavorting in their Jacuzzis, sipping champagne, and tickling one another with peacock feathers. Once
again, the pleasures of communal bathing were extolled. The *New York
Times* summed up this aspect of the 1970s: "In an era when self-absorption
was elevated to the status of a national pastime, what could have been
more appropriate than the turning of one's daily cleansing into a rite?"

Circular shower, Aix-les-Bains, France.

Compulsive bathing is sometimes indicative of a psychopathic personality. Hitler, for example, required a shampoo, fresh underwear, and two baths a day. He endured intense trauma when he could not wash his fingers after greeting a stranger.

During this period the bathroom really came into its own; famous designers began producing fancy towels and shower curtains, bathroom fixtures, elaborate tiles, special shower heads, plexiglass sliding shower doors, bathside telephones, and a huge array of bath toys. It was estimated that the average American took more than seven baths or showers a week.

In contemporary American culture, suppression of body smells has become a virtue; frequent bathing is supplemented by perfumes and deodorants to hide even a hint of what might be considered a human smell. In 1990, $500 million were spent on bath products in the United States.

In 1986, *Psychology Today* published an article attributing family stress to too few bathrooms in the home. Washing had become such a private ritual that people resisted sharing their facilities even with the people closest to them. According to the article, if there were not enough bathrooms, family members would suffer. In a short time, the number of bathrooms per capita began to increase, sometimes exceeding the number of bedrooms in the house.

In the 1990s, bathing has become very leisurely and convivial; we may well outstrip the Romans in savoring its pleasures. Putting the fun back into bathing is certainly one way of accomplishing the resurrection of the body. Bathtubs and bathrooms are made of many materials, from marble to limestone to acrylic. Bathroom accoutrements, including TVs, videos, dressing rooms, and oversize Jacuzzis, are proliferating at an amazing rate. One of the most recent products is a "sensorium," a bath/whirlpool with controls for presetting water temperature and lighting that can be activated from a car phone, so that it will be ready by the time one gets home.

The value of bathing as a stress-reducing element has long been recognized. The hot water and the relaxation seem to affect problem solving. Winston Churchill, for example, took two baths a day to relax and clear his mind. Many authors confess to writing while soaking in a tub—a tradition that dates back at least to Edmond Rostand and Benjamin Franklin. Rostand took refuge in a bathtub and wrote there all day, producing such classics as *Cyrano de Bergerac* (1897). Agatha Christie took hot baths and sniffed fermenting green apples to stimulate her muse. Richard Wagner soaked in a tub scented with Milk of Iris perfume for several hours a day while working on *Parsifal* (1882). In *The Natural History of the Senses,* Diane Ackerman points out that writing is a spiritual activity that makes one completely forget, temporarily, that one has a body. "It is the disturbance of the balance of the body and mind and for this reason one needs a kind of anchor of sensation with the physical world," wrote English poet Stephen Spender in his essay "Making a Poem." Water displaces 90 percent of one's body weight, creating a sensation of lightness. Also, when the temperature of the water and the body converge, the mind feels free to travel. No wonder Archimedes is said to have jumped out of the tub stark naked and run through the streets of Syracuse shouting, "Eureka, eureka!" (I have found it!). Lying in the tub, he had discovered that a body immersed in liquid displaces weight equal to its own weight. In the bath, anything can happen.

Japanese Baths and Hot Springs

A hot-spring bath can cure anything but love.
Kusatsu folk song

While Europe and the Middle East were writing their bath history, Japan was discovering its own resources. Perched gingerly upon the Ring of Fire, the volcanic islands of Japan have some twenty thousand bubbling hot springs; steam and water gush and spray almost everywhere. It is a visual delight: some springs are bloodred and naturally scented with hibiscus, while others are milky white and foul-smelling.

The Japanese regard their springs as sacred gifts from the gods and from the earth, and there are frequent allusions to springs in their creation myths. Rituals, such as the presentation of hot water to the shrine spirits in Nasu Yumoto spring, evolved out of reverence for these special waters.

Animals played a great part in discovering the healing properties of Japan's thermal waters. Legends are full of beasts and birds rolling about in sulfurous mud and steam to heal their wounds. From the graceful heron to the clumsy bear, they mysteriously found their way to the special waters to relieve their ailments. Later these animals, revered as water deities, were enshrined at different springs.

In northern Japan, monkeys sit and relax in steaming outdoor pools surrounded by snowy rocks as the chilly wind whistles about and ice rolls down to the edge of the pools, melting into the water. They have discovered a way to keep warm through the cold winters and to derive pleasure from it at the same time. In the south, other monkeys chatter and steal towels from people at the hot springs.

The Japanese had perfected the art of cleanliness by the time Western explorers arrived on the islands. Frequent references to the obsessive cleanliness of the Japanese can be found in Chinese historical records dating as far back as the third century A.D.

Personal hygiene and ritual purification have played an important part in Japanese culture; purity of body and spirit is an integral part of the Shinto religion. When Buddhism was introduced to the islands in A.D. 552, its tenets combined neatly with the Shinto idea of spiritual cleansing through immersion. By taking a bath, the bather would not only purge the body of its sins but also have seven times better luck in every other respect. The baths in Kyoto, Nara, and Nakamura were established as annexes to centers of Buddhism as a means of attracting converts; later, commercial baths were established.

Buddhist and Shinto priests, roaming the mountains in search of sacred spots where they could meditate, discovered new springs. They were often guided to these sources by mysterious spirits who appeared in their dreams and meditations. Samurai, daimyos, and even shoguns also had their favorite waters, which they reserved for their soldiers, much as the Romans did while conquering their way through Europe.

LEFT: *Katsushika Hokusai,* Women at a Public Bath, *page from the* Manga, *vol. 1, early nineteenth century, woodblock print. The Metropolitan Museum of Art, New York, the Howard Mansfield Collection. Gift of Howard Mansfield, 1936.*

RIGHT: *Japanese women in cable-car baths, Arita hot springs, Japan.*

So-called charity baths further linked the bath with the temple. Empress Koyo, who lived during the eighth century, is often portrayed leaning over and washing the gnarled body of an elderly person, her voluminous black hair cascading to the floor; after her death she was made the saint of charity baths. During this period it also became customary for hosts to bathe their guests, since purging other people's afflictions of body and soul was considered an act of great charity.

Bathhouses became part of Japanese social life around the seventh century. Initially, they resembled Finnish baths: wood was burned until the embers glowed and then salt water was poured on them, creating the steam for a bath. In the next stage of development, vats containing water were placed underneath a platform constructed on stilts. When the water came to a boil, the steam rose and the bather, sitting or reclining on the platform, relaxed in the hot mist.

Communal bathhouses became gathering places, especially for the working classes, who wanted a place where they could shed problems and connect with friends, as a Japanese proverb emphasizes: *Hadaka to hadaka no tsukiai* (bathing buddies are the best of friends). But class distinctions created a problem. To cope with the chaos of mixing the classes, bathhouse owners devised separate entrances and pools, but they did not segregate the sexes. Although men and women occasionally peeked at each other, Japanese baths apparently did not develop into the scandalous, orgiastic baths of Rome or medieval Europe. A man could ask to have a woman bathe him and perform sexual favors, but this would always be done in a private part of the bathhouse. In the meantime men and women continued to bathe communally, and families bathed together with their children. It was a natural, everyday activity; there was no shame in nudity.

In 1853 "shame" arrived in Japan in the guise of Commodore Matthew Perry, who was mortified at the sight of naked men and women bathing in public. By the 1870s mixed bathing was prohibited by law. Segregated quarters were established in most bathhouses, but sometimes the only thing separating the sexes was a log or a rope installed just to please the inspectors.

By the mid-1800s there were more than five hundred bathhouses, or *yuya,* in Edo (Tokyo) and thousands more around the country. At the turn of this century, Tokyo boasted a thousand bathhouses, and half a million people used them every day, sometimes twice a day.

Japanese baths were always very hot, ideally around 110 degrees Fahrenheit, much hotter than most Westerners are accustomed to. People washed and rinsed before entering the pools, in order not to pollute them. They stayed in the water as long as they could endure the heat, before drying themselves with damp towels. At the Kusatsu hot springs, an interesting bath called the time bath is offered. Attendants stir and beat the water rhythmically with long boards, singing until it is ready. The water is so hot that the bathers make out their wills before getting in. Once submerged, they are allowed to scream, curse, swear—whatever they need to do to combat the heat. The object is to stay in the water for exactly three minutes. Those who succeed emerge looking like boiled lobsters but recover rather quickly and go into the cool pools. The practice of *yudedako,* which literally means "boiled octopus," is considered essential for achieving perfect physical well-being and is a cure for a whole range of corporeal and emotional problems. It is also thought to be a necessity for the attainment of mental serenity and the Shinto version of enlightenment.

In Japan, although the bath experience is communal and enjoyable, it is approached with a serious attitude. To the Romans, the bath prepared and refreshed the bather for an activity after the bath. For the Japanese the bath, generally taken at night, heals the wounds incurred during the day and relaxes the bather for sleep. The prevalence of bathing arises from a deeply entrenched psychological need in the Japanese mind.

During the twentieth century the popularity of *onsen* (thermal springs) in Japan increased as the bullet train and buses made travel easier. Hordes of businessmen flocked to some sixteen hundred *onsen* spas for R&R. Just like their nineteenth-century European predecessors, these spas became fashionable resorts offering luxurious accommodations and entertainment, with geishas puttering around lighting cigarettes, singing, dancing, and flattering.

Some *onsen* maintained their traditional medicinal aspects, but while continuing to practice the holistic philosophy of attaining an equilibrium of mind and body, they introduced Western concepts of rest, exercise, and diet into their programs. These places came to be called *kuahausu,* derived from the German *Kurhaus* ("cure house," spa building).

The Japanese have also devised all sorts of ingenious ways to take the waters. On Honshu's Wakayama Peninsula, for example, one entrepreneur channeled a hot spring into a mountain cable car, making it possible to sit in a tub while flying over a gorge.

One of the most popular *onsen* is Beppu, in northeastern Kyushu. The attraction of its springs can be traced back to a Shinto deity named Sukunahiko, who suffered from an acute illness until another deity plunged him into the Beppu hot spring, whereupon Sukunahiko was instantly revived. So began the pilgrimages. A ninth-century document described the benefits of Beppu as follows: "You take a dip in it, and you look more attractive than ever. You take another, and you suffer from no illnesses for the rest of your life." Beppu attracted not only the Japanese but a roster of Western celebrities, including George Bernard Shaw and Charlie Chaplin.

Beppu probably has the most impressive geophysics of all the *onsen* resorts. The colored boiling ponds called *jigoku* (hells) are vermilion, emerald, and blue, owing to the different minerals in the water, and as the colors merge and separate again they create weird and wonderful surreal effects. One of the most exotic facilities is a pit filled with coffee grounds in which people are buried up to the neck, not unlike *fango* (volcanic ash) baths. The treatment is supposed to be energizing.

Today the Japanese continue to enjoy the pleasures of communal bathing and are often thought of as "ofuroholics," or bath fanatics. Every year an estimated one hundred million people check in at a hot-spring *ryokan* (inn). As a guidebook puts it, "Their passion for hot bathing is proverbial, and no other people in the world take such pride in their sanitary arrangements." As the adage goes, "Americans bathe to get clean; Japanese get clean to bathe." For the Japanese, hot springs are not simply an infatuation but a lifelong love affair.

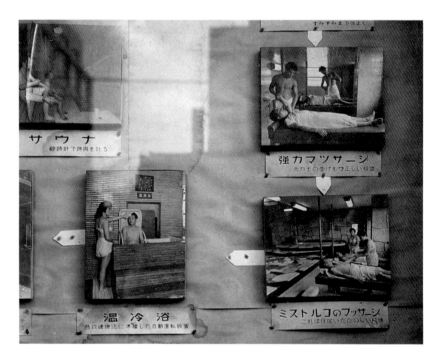

Advertisement for a Japanese bathhouse, Tokyo.

*Incredible these halls of water. They are the only fairy lands which subsist on earth.
In two months, more happens there than in the rest of the universe during the rest of
the year. One could truly say that the sources are not mineralized, but sourcerized.*
GUY DE MAUPASSANT, *Mont-Oriol: A Spa Romance*

European Spas

Aesculapius

*Come ye Naiads! to the fountains lead!
Propitious maids! the task remains to sing
Your gifts (so Praeon [Aesculapius], so the powers of Health
Command), to praise your crystal element.
O Comfortable streams! with eager lips
And trembling hands the languid thirsty quaff
New life in you; fresh vigor fills their veins.*
ARMSTRONG, *Art of Preserving Health*

Besides being a powerful cure for physical ailments, water also played an effective role in the field of psychotherapy. Aesculapius, the god of *nootherapeia*, or mind healing, who rose in status during the plague of 293 B.C., utilized bathing as an effective means of dispelling not only physical but also mental illness. The centers of Aesculapius, whose practices were reputed to purify and integrate mind, body, and spirit, spread from the town of Epidaurus across the Greek, Egyptian, and later Roman worlds. Here Hippocrates and other early physicians used methods that went out of vogue for almost two millenniums but are now once again finding their way into the world of healing. They practiced dream therapy, for example,

Sir Edward John Poynter, A Visit to Aesculapius, *1880, oil on canvas, 59½ x 90 in. (151.1 x 228.6 cm). Tate Gallery, London*

whereby the patients were asked to tell their dreams after sleeping their first night in the center at Epidaurus.

Since an important part of the Aesculapian practice was the use of water, the centers were often built close to natural springs. Aesculapian priests bathed people in these springs or sometimes in the sea and pre-scribed "taking the waters," which they considered sacred. There is a foun-tain in the Aesculapian center on the island of Kos that was believed to cure nervous ailments but could cause panic if a person drank from it without believing in its powers.

Early Spas

In the beginning, spas were simply wells, pools, or mineral springs thought to be endowed with magical healing abilities; they offered spiritual as well as physical cures. The afflicted, who had no other hope, made pilgrimages to them seeking remedies. How they were healed was a mystery, but the cure was often attributed to strange forces in the water rather than to the water itself. Water thus became a vehicle for divine healing, as John Lydgate expressed in his fifteenth-century *Falls of Princes:*

> *These bathes to soften sinews haue*
> *Great vertue and scoure the skin;*
> *From morphew white, and blacke to saue,*
> *The bodies faint, are bathde therein.*
>
> *From leprye, scabs, and sores are olde,*
> *For scurfes, and botche, and humors fall,*

> *The bathes haue vertues many folde,*
> *If God giue grace to cure them all.*

At first, no one cared how fancy the accommodations were, provided that the waters were effective. Gradually, as the number of guests increased, spas became commercialized: often the owner of the land on which a spring was located would provide accommodations for those who came to take advantage of its miraculous powers; in turn, he took their money.

> *Here are your waters and your watering places*
> *Drink and be whole again beyond confusion.*
> ROBERT FROST, "Directive"

The Roman invaders' addiction to bathing sanctified certain springs. Julius Caesar quenched his thirst and later built the baths at Vicus Calidus (hot town), know to us as Vichy. Aquae Sulis (Bath) in England had an enormous temple dedicated to Minerva. In Germany, the spring that the Romans called Aquae Aureliae became Baden-Baden (bath bath). Both Perrier in the south of France and Ferralelle in southern Italy boast that Hannibal and his armies sampled their effervescences.

> *Some drink of it, and in an houre,*
> *Their Stomach, Guts, and Kidneys scower:*
> *Others doe Bathe, and ulcers cure,*
> *Dry Itch, and Leprosie impure;*
> *And what in Lords you call the Gout,*
> *In poor the Pox, this drives all out.*
> "To a Friend upon a Journey to Epsom
>   Well," in *Musarum Deliciae* (1655)

The most thriving spas were elaborate temples dedicated to the gods of water and built around natural springs. They varied according to the type of water. There are basically three kinds: saline waters contain dissolved salts such as Epsom salts (named after the mineral springs in Epsom, England), or magnesium sulfate, used primarily for its purgative effects. Chalybeate waters, characterized by the rust-colored iron oxide produced when ferrous carbonate is exposed to air, contain different kinds of iron salts and have tonic and restorative effects. Finally, sulfur waters contain hydrogen sulfide—the same gas given off by rotten eggs—which is primarily used for bathing or drinking and to treat the skin.

Other variables were the temperature and the degree of natural effervescence. Since these water cocktails provided limitless possibilities for doctors, it was a matter of personal opinion which ones to prescribe. Specialists devised a number of complex internal and external water cures, and people took their word for it.

Spa Pilgrims

Historical luminaries attributed their own recovery to particular springs and endorsed them. Michel de Montaigne, for example, set out for Rome in 1580, seeking both pleasure and cure. He stopped along the way at the baths of La Villa in Tuscany. "I went back to drinking that [water] of the ordinary spring, and took five pounds of it," he wrote. "It did not induce me to sweat, as it used to do. The first time I passed some of the water I discharged some gravel, which seemed in fact to be broken up stones. . . . It had a good effect in both directions; and it was lucky that I did not believe those doctors who ordered me to give up drinking."

"I am much better than I have been," wrote Michelangelo. "Morning and evening I have been drinking the water from a spring about forty miles from Rome (Fiuggi), which breaks up my kidney stone. . . . I have had to lay in a supply at home and cannot drink or cook with anything else."

Elizabeth I believed in the benefits of bathing and sometimes sent her courtiers to the watering holes. One of the most notable early patrons of Buxton was Mary Queen of Scots; she frequently visited the place between 1573 and 1584 to cure her rheumatism, while she was in the custody of the Earl of Shrewsbury. Shortly before her death the ill-fated queen wrote the following nostalgic couplet in Latin:

> *Buxton, whose fame thy milk-warm waters tell,*
> *Whom I, perhaps, no more shall see, farewell!*

In the seventeenth century Celia Fiennes, a British lady-in-waiting and an intrepid water drinker, had an insatiable urge to sample all the different spas in England. Fortunately for posterity, this tenacious traveler left behind a gem of a guidebook, extolling the vices and virtues of a variety of seventeenth-century water establishments.

In 1697 she wrote of Buxton, "the beer they allowe at the meales is so bad that very little can be dranke . . . the Lodgings so bad, 2 beds in room some 3 beds and some 4 in one roome . . . and sometymes they are so crowded that three must lye in bed. . . . We staid two nights by reason one of our company was ill but it was sore against our wills." Of the spa at Astrop (1694): "much frequented by the Gentry. . . . there was a Gravell walke that is between 2 high cutt hedges where there is a room for the Musick and Roome for the Company besides a Private Walkes." In Bristol the water was "exceeding clear and warm as new milk and much of that sweetness." And in Low Harrogate, "the Sulphur or stincking Spaw is not completely termed for the smell being so strong and offensive that I could not force my horse near the well."

Daniel Defoe also expressed antipathy for the baths: "The smoke and the slime of the waters, the promiscuous multitude of the people in the bath, with nothing but their heads above water, with the height of the walls that environ the bath, gave me a lively idea of the several pictures I had seen of Fra Angelico's in Italy of Purgatory, with heads and hands uplifted in the midst of smoke, just as they are here."

Madame de Sévigné found the baths equally objectionable. "I started to shower this morning and it is a great rehearsal for purgatory," she wrote in 1676, describing the baths in Vichy. "One is completely nude in this little underground place and there one finds a tube with hot water that a woman aims at different parts of her body. It is a very humiliating thing."

The people who turned spa life into literature became known as "water poets." Spas most definitely inspired versifiers—some quite pathetic but others even prophetic. Some mixed faith and pathos with humor:

> *Here lies I and my three daughters*
> *Died from drinking the Cheltenham waters,*
> *If we had stuck to Epsom salts,*
> *We shouldn't be lying in these cold vaults.*

In their marriage contracts young girls requested the privilege to go to the spas without their husbands, so that they could enjoy themselves freely. Nuns took off their habits when they visited the spas. The Church was unable to discourage the progression toward "steamier times." People got into trouble when they got into hot water.

Medicine Enters Spas

The Reformation brought about an important change. Once the spirits were no longer credited with mystical powers, holy wells became wishing wells. As the spirits were neglected, faith went out and doctors came in. The spas were cleaned up once again, and the public returned in search of a new nostrum.

Cleanliness improved general health conditions. Paracelsus and other forerunners of modern medicine attributed the cures not to anything supernatural but to the physical constitution of the elements, yet they still endorsed the healing properties of certain springs. Nothing could discredit waters deemed efficient since prehistoric times.

"The morning when the Sunne is an houre more or lesse high, is the fittest time to drinke the water," wrote one of the most renowned early doctors, Lodwick Rowsee, in his book *Queenes Welles* (1632). "For when the Sunne beginneth to be of force, it doth attract some of the mineral spirits and the water loses some of its strength."

Doctors believed that there was no complaint for which nature had not devised a cure in the form of some kind of chemical solution. The list was like the litany of the physicians in Molière's *Le Malade imaginaire*. Medicine was no longer a blend of alchemy and magic but a science based on knowledge and recommendations for types of bathing, couched in the legitimate language of science. In essence, spas became hospitals.

People were encouraged to drink waters with a high mineral content in order to cure everything from kidney stones to heart trouble. Enormous quantities of water—sometimes exceeding two hundred ounces a day—often with offensive smells, were prescribed for drinking. Folk songs and

poems claimed that hot springs could cure anything but love; some claimed to cure even that.

> The brand she quenched in a cool well by,
> Which from Love's fire took heat perpetual,
> Growing a bath and healthful remedy
> For men diseased. But I, my mistress' thrall,
>   Came there for cure, and this by that I prove,
> Love's fire heats water, water cools not love.
> SHAKESPEARE, "Sonnet 154"

Woman being carried to the baths, Aix-les-Bains, France.

As the reputation of the healing potential of certain springs grew, so did a more demanding clientele. The aristocracy and the rich, dissipated by their overindulgent life-style, were sold on the virtues of these springs, but they wanted to take the waters in the manner to which they were accustomed. After all, it was no better to die of boredom than of constipation. They required fine accommodations, facilities, and entertainment and were willing to pay for it. Clever entrepreneurs saw this as a golden opportunity to take advantage of the finer needs of the privileged class and created dreamlike environments around special springs. By the middle of the nineteenth century, these spas had become the ultimate in architectural excess, as well as the playpen of the rich. Spa history was reinvented.

TOP: *Women's baths, Saint-Amand-les-Eaux, France.*

CENTER: *Shower and massage, Vichy, France, ca. 1900.*

BOTTOM: *The park at the Baignots spa, France.*

Spa Society

From the moment the old Roman baths were revived in the nineteenth century until the 1930s, spa fever infected Europe. To satisfy their water longings, people took to the roads in great numbers. Some bathing facilities became so crowded that, to accommodate the overflow of customers, they were often open all night long.

These cities of water became the rendezvous of the greatest minds and beauties of the world, who came seeking to rid themselves of their afflictions while languishing in the pleasure of the waters and enjoying the stimulation of high culture. A new society was born: the water society.

Intimacy was much more possible when people shared a common experience of rejuvenation, transcendence, and rebirth. The waters created a great synergy between material and spiritual states, satisfying the hunger of the soul as well as of the flesh. Taking the waters healed not only the body but the mind as well. In the watering places time ran backward slowly, opening up infinite channels of creativity. Miracles and dreams became tangible. Taking the waters was a means of unleashing creative urges for painters, writers, and composers. Spa literature and spa music virtually oozed out of the fountains.

The therapeutic decadence of spa life was a forbidden nostrum for curing Victorian prudery. The potent fountains became projections of health, beauty, and prosperity, but more than anything, sex.

The roster of visitors to such places goes far back in history and includes such famous names as Julius Caesar, Michelangelo, Montaigne, Casanova, Napoleon and Josephine, Queen Victoria, Victor Hugo, Flaubert, Berlioz, Goethe, Turgenev, Tolstoy, Dostoyevsky, Henry James, Agatha Christie, and countless others. Napoleon went to Vichy; George Frederick Handel to Aix-la-Chapelle. Queen Victoria preferred Aix-les-Bains. Empress Josephine spent endless hours sitting on a vaporous hole at Plombiers—whose waters

Louis XVI room, Konversationshaus, Baden-Baden, Germany.

were famous for curing infertility—in hopes of giving an heir to Napoleon. Beethoven and Goethe took the waters at Carlsbad, which claimed to have cured more illnesses, including occult disorders, than any other spa in Europe. Turgenev snubbed Dostoyevsky in Baden-Baden, and Dostoyevsky was crushed to be so humiliated by the author he most admired.

Railroads enabled the wealthy and famous to travel to their favorite watering holes at will. To satisfy the finer needs of these luminaries, grand hotels were built with casinos, theaters, and marble drinking halls, where the elegant clientele sipped water from Lalique glasses. At night, cotillions facilitated encounters that would lead to important romantic affairs, business deals, or political alliances. Spa towns were transformed into a dreamland for snobs and fortune hunters.

The French discovered that gambling was a perfect accompaniment to taking the waters, and the English were attracted to both the baths and the tables. The Russians had their own stylish spas in the Caucasus, such as Pyatigorsk, the playground of the St. Petersburg crowd, but apparently their glamour was fading by the middle of the nineteenth century, at least in the eyes of the jaded protagonist of Mikhail Lermontov's novel *A Hero of Our Time* (1840): "Our life here is rather prosaic. Those who drink the waters in the morning are insipid like all invalids, and those who drink wine in the evening are unbearable like all healthy people. Feminine society exists, but there is little comfort therein: these ladies play whist, dress badly and speak dreadful French!" European spas, especially the German ones, also had great appeal for the Russian aristocracy.

Opulence abounded in these water towns. Some of the privileged class built their own beautiful villas and chose their neighbors. During the day they took the water cures—treatments that promised youth, beauty, and a cure for every conceivable illness. The proprietors and doctors concocted creative new devices and strenuous forms of hydrotherapy—dripping sheet baths, douche baths, gargling baths, rain baths, sitz baths, vapor baths, sulfur baths, deluge baths, slime baths. Nineteenth-century cartoons portrayed spa goers in an assortment of torture chambers. But if taking the cure itself was often an ordeal, life after dark was elegant and refined. Stylish women could be seen strolling under parasols on the arms of distinguished-looking men. It was a time for dining, dancing, and gambling.

European royalty endowed their favorite healing springs with monumental edifices, the grandeur of which few public buildings today can eclipse. In *Villes d'eaux en France* (1985), an impressive catalog of an exhibition of French water villages, John-Michel Belorgey describes the range: "Neo-Classic, neo-Renaissance, neo-Palladian, neo-Byzantine, neo-Mooresque, neo-Babylonian, neo-Egyptian, neo-Flemish, neo-Venetian, exotic, vernacular, neo-Norman." In other words, stupefyingly eclectic. He perceives spa architecture as "a great cry of somewhat corrupted joie de vivre."

The Romans could hardly have imagined that, millenniums later, their baths would be transformed into the most splendid palaces of healing. These nineteenth-century water palaces possessed a kind of splendor that no longer exists, but when visiting them today, it is impossible not to feel the ghosts of the spa goers of a bygone era or to ignore the strata of history embedded in their architecture.

The Legendary Spas

ENGLAND

Bath

In 1727 workmen digging a sewer trench in the town of Bath, England, discovered a remarkable, life-size gilded bronze head of Minerva, the Roman goddess of wisdom. It belonged to the cult statue of the deity that once stood on a pedestal inside a temple. Its discovery was a prelude to an amazing unfolding of history that still continues. Over the years the temple was excavated, including the original Roman baths, which presented a template for a whole way of life.

The springs of Bath were first used by Paleolithic hunters seven thousand years ago. Later they became an important site for the Celts, who believed them to be sacred to their goddess Sulis.

Around 800 B.C. an apocryphal prince named Blaudad was banished from his father's kingdom after contracting leprosy. During his years of wandering, Blaudad became a swineherd and, much to his dismay, noticed that his animals were contracting his disease. One day he observed the pigs scampering down a hill and wallowing in some hot springs. Before long they became well again. When Blaudad realized that their recovery was somehow connected to the springs, he himself plunged into the steaming swamp. This wallow was at the source of Bath's thermal springs. Blaudad was cured of leprosy and returned to reclaim his kingdom, building his capital around the springs, which he named Caer Baden. He also reputedly sired King Lear!

The steaming waters of Caer Baden thrilled the Romans when they arrived in A.D. 76. At the main spring (now called the King's Bath), they found an ancient Celtic shrine to Sulis, so they renamed the town Aquae Sulis. Conflating Sulis with Minerva, the Romans built their own shrine on the site, which they called the temple of Sulis Minerva. This Corinthian-style complex encompassed Roman baths and a theater for religious as well as secular performances. The temple, the spa, and the theater formed the nucleus of a great social and spiritual center that dominated the town for four centuries.

TOP: *The Pavillon Springs, Contrexéville, France.*

BOTTOM: *The Salle de Gargarisme, Vichy, France.*

Allier — 206 - VICHY, le Gargarisme

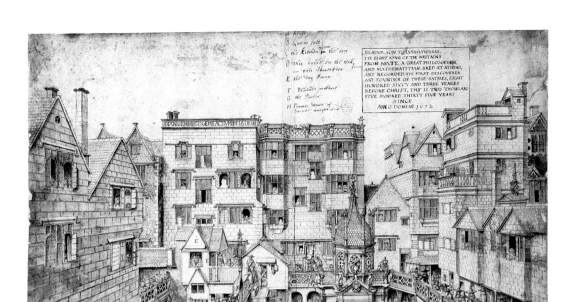

The King's Bath spring, in the center of Bath, bubbles out of the ground at the rate of a quarter of a million gallons a day, maintaining a constant temperature of 46.5 degrees Celsius (120 degrees Fahrenheit). The source of its water is rain that fell about ten thousand years ago and penetrated deep into the earth, where it was warmed by the natural heat of the earth's core. To the Romans the spring was not merely a source of hot water but a sacred place where mortals could communicate with the deities of the underworld—a tradition that has its roots in pagan well worship. It attracted droves of people seeking the assistance of Minerva.

An important function of the sacred spring was to bring retribution to one's enemy. If a person felt persecuted in some way—for example, if his/her shoes had been stolen—he/she would go to the temple scribe and compose a letter to the goddess, usually following a standard form written in a kind of legal language, as for instance: "May he who stole my shoes, whether he be man or woman, boy or girl, freedman or slave, become impotent and die. It may have been [the name of the suspect]."

After the message was composed, it was inscribed on a sheet of pewter and thrown into the spring. Because no one wanted to have his or her name scratched on the infamous pewter scrolls and fall out of grace with Minerva, people were obliged to maintain a higher moral standard.

Recovered from the spring in modern times, the Bath curses are extraordinary documents, not only reflecting the petty irritations of everyday

Thomas Johnson,
The King and
Queen's Bath, *1672,*
pen and ink with
gray wash, 13⅞ x 18½
in. (33.5 x 47 cm).
Courtesy of the Trust-
ees of the British
Museum

life but also giving us a glimpse into the hopes, expectations, and piety of a society during four hundred years of Roman occupation. We also gain insight into its sacred means of crime control.

Besides the Bath curses, an astounding number of coins were discovered in the spring, so many that it seems a cash offering to the deity was de rigueur in return for favors granted or offerings made. The temptation to throw coins into a fountain and make a wish is obviously a universal and timeless human practice. Archaeologists also excavated a pair of dice among the ruins; they were loaded.

The buildings of the temple fell into disrepair after the Romans left in the fourth century, and the city was gradually enclosed within walls. We have very little evidence of what happened during the Dark Ages, but the mere fact that Bath became known as an *akemanceaster* (sick man's town) suggests that people continued taking the waters. There are rumors of people with leprosy, scabies, and open wounds sloshing about in the hot waters, with a few cats and dogs thrown in for fun.

In the early twelfth century the monks of Bath refurbished the spring as a bath, which they called the King's Bath, named after Henry I. They carved niches in the inner face of the existing Roman wall to shelter the bathers. Patrons had the privilege of having personal prayers written for them by the local bishop, who controlled the King's Bath and dictated its

John Ronayne, The Sacred Spring Reconstructed, *1986, watercolor, 19 x 14 in. (48.3 x 35.6 cm). Bath Archaeological Trust, England*

social and moral code. In 1559 the bishop issued stricter codes of conduct, because reports of scandalous behavior had increased. He decreed, for example, that anyone who had reached puberty was required to wear a robe while bathing, whereas before, people had entered the water naked. Another bishop preached: "God must heal the waters before they have any virtue to heal you."

Men and women shared the baths. The women wore voluminous gowns that filled with water, and carried trays holding their snuffboxes, flowers, and sal volatile—aromatic smelling salts.

During the Renaissance the best-known baths were the King's Bath, the Cross Bath, and the Hot Bath, all built above hot springs. When Elizabeth I visited Bath in 1574, they were all open-air structures and she was so appalled by the smell that she turned around and left. Toward the end of the sixteenth century a new bathhouse, exclusively for women, was constructed.

Anne of Denmark, wife of James I, visited the women's bath in the early seventeenth century, seeking a cure for gout and dropsy. Apparently she did not mind the smell and took to the waters immediately. Her enthusiasm generated such great publicity that this bath became known as the Queen's Bath and survived until the Victorian era, when it was demolished in order to excavate more of the Roman ruins.

"It cannot be clean to have so many bodies in the same water," commented Samuel Pepys, who never took a bath in his life. By the seventeenth century, while many European spas prospered, Bath had become somewhat unsavory, accommodating mostly the common people, while some of the aristocracy sought watering holes elsewhere.

Despite these deterrents, in 1663 Charles II took his wife, Catherine of Braganza, to Bath to cure her infertility. The waters did not have the desired effect on Catherine, but Mary of Modena, wife of James II, who visited the spa in 1687, was more fortunate. Nine months after her stay, she gave birth to a royal son.

Bath reached the height of its grandeur during the eighteenth century, thanks to Beau Nash, who came to the spa as a master of ceremonies in 1705 and presided over its social life for fifty-five years. During Nash's reign, Bath was hailed as one of the most elegant spas in Europe. In *The New Bath Guide,* poet Christopher Ansley sang Nash's praises:

> *For this, in compassion to mortals below,*
> *The gods, their peculiar favour to shew,*
> *Sent Hermes to Bath in the shape of a Beau.*

Nash knew how to keep the beggars at bay and had sedan-chair carriers at the visitors' beck and call. By serving breakfast and afternoon tea, and providing music and spa water, he restored Bath's elegance. A man of good taste, he imposed manners on the social life at Bath, prohibiting swearing, carrying swords, and wearing top boots. He insisted that aprons were for serving wenches, not for ladies, and forbade women to wear them; he carried out the edict by tearing the apron off the Duchess of Queensberry at a ball. Nash lived in a beautiful mansion and inspired the spa's developers to build fine accommodations, exquisite terraces, crescents, and circuses. The whole town was constructed in an airy classicism by architect Joseph Wood and his son, turning Bath into an architectural jewel.

By 1708 Nash had devised a comprehensive fitness program that attracted more visitors than ever to the spa. The day began with a bath in the hot springs between 6:00 and 9:00 A.M., followed by a drinking of the waters in the pump room to a musical accompaniment. Breakfast was then served, and in the early afternoon visitors had the option of attending a service in the abbey. After that, everyone was free to do as they pleased— nap, shop, write letters—until 3:00 P.M., when dinner was served. A postprandial stroll culminated in a return to the pump room and more water. In the evenings, tea was followed by some sort of entertainment, often gambling.

"The gaming is worthy of the decline of an Empire," wrote Horace Walpole in 1770. Pugilism and gambling were two sports that greatly appealed to eighteenth-century men. They would bet on anything—horses, cocks, dogs, even the life expectancies of certain people. One man bet on how long a person could stay under water, hired a hobo, sank and drowned him, then hired another and tried the same.

In 1714 Alexander Pope, who was generally difficult to please, wrote in a letter: "Slid, I can't tell how, into all the Amusements of this Place: My whole day is shar'd by the Pump-Assemblies, the Walkes, the Chocolate houses, Raffling Shops, Plays, Medleys &c."

Above the entrance to the baths was a sign that read, WATER IS BEST. Charles Dickens did not agree. He said that it tasted like "drinking warm irons." Instead, he took his wife to Malvern for a cold-water cure and found, "a good deal in it. . . . My experience of that treatment induces me to hold that it is wonderously efficacious where there is constitutional vitality; where there is not, I think it may be a little questionable."

The town drew high rollers. Observed novelist Tobias Smollett in 1771: "Clerks and factors from the East . . . planters, negro-drivers, and hucksters from American plantations. . . . Usurers, brokers, and robbers of every kind; men of low birth, and no breeding . . . without taste or conduct . . . all of them hurry to Bath, because here, without any further qualification, they can mingle with the princes and nobles."

Seldom did a day pass without some sort of scandal. The upper and lower classes mingled freely, as is portrayed in Jane Austen's *Northanger Abbey* (1818). During the Regency the baths became places where the sexes seductively displayed themselves to each other with undisguised ebullience. In *Lettres d'un Français,* Abbé Le Blanc describes the transformation young women went through after visiting Bath: "They became new creatures, casting off the constraint and melancholy imposed upon them by the yoke of habit during the rest of the year in the Capital, and for one glorious and by no means virtuous month enjoyed a water cure that was as primitive in fact as in appearance—by artfully calculated deception—it was made to look civilized."

Charles Dickens, William Makepeace Thackeray, Fanny Burney, and Jane Austen all found inspiration in Bath. Sir Thomas Gainsborough kept a

ABOVE: *The bathhouse, Bath, England.*

LEFT: *The source, Bath, England.*

studio there for fourteen years and painted a great deal. Emma Hamilton worked there as a maid, and Lord Nelson frequently came to take the waters between campaigns.

But after the Victorian era, Bath lost its fine, carefree spirit and became a respectable watering place with solid-looking hotels, bathhouses, and fleets of big black bath chairs. Attendance never declined, however, because after World War II the spa was subsidized by the British government's free health service. But in 1976 its doors were closed to the public. This was a blessing in disguise, because shortly afterward an excavating team discovered that the spring was contaminated with amoebic meningitis; it had to be cleaned out and all the pipes replaced. It was a difficult but necessary task, and the baths remained closed for more than a decade, but now they are open once again.

FRANCE

In France and most other European countries *thermalisme* (thermal healing) is taken so seriously that it is taught as a course in medical schools. The French government prescribes spa treatments to around a million people a year. Each person is assigned to a spa for the particular cure it offers. One of the most outstanding water cures that the French have developed is thalassotherapy, which uses seawater. Such seaside resorts as Deauville, La Baule, Quiberon, and Biarritz specialize in this revitalizing treatment.

Evian-les-Bains

One of the most memorable events of my life was going to the village square in Evian, a small town on the southern shore of Lake Geneva, with three empty bottles and filling them with Evian water directly from its source. It gave me a peculiar sense of timelessness and of identification with the people who, since ancient times, have gathered at village squares to fill their bottles from fountains, to talk, and to gossip. It was odd to think that I could be sitting in a restaurant anywhere in the world and drinking the same water that came from this very source.

In Evian, water is everywhere—in the serenity of the lake, in the gushing mountain streams and waterfalls, and of course in the spring itself. You imbibe it as often as you breathe; you are power-hosed with it, massaged under it, and steamed by it, all for your well-being.

The discovery of Evian also dates back to ancient times. We know that Roman emperor Flavius Claudius Jovianus passed through the area in A.D. 363 on his way to Germany. We also know that in the Middle Ages people traveled far to reach the source. But the real story begins in 1789, while France was in the throes of revolution. The marquis de Lessert, a nobleman who was suffering from kidney stones, went to a small spa in Amphion, near Evian, to take the waters. While wandering in the countryside one day, the marquis sampled some water from a spring in the garden of a certain Monsieur Cachat. It was light and refreshing, and he kept returning for more. After a while his kidney stones disappeared.

This incident attracted authorities who tested and approved the spring. Evian water came to be credited with easing the discomfort of kidney stones by disintegrating gravel buildup. Because it had a very low and constant mineral composition and was low in sodium, it also appealed to those suffering from high blood pressure. Crowds gathered to sample the water. As for Monsieur Cachat, he fenced in his spring and sold its water.

ABOVE: *Thermal establishment, Evian-les-Bains, France.*

RIGHT: *Anna de Noailles.*

The spa in Evian was established by 1815, but its golden age did not begin until the turn of the twentieth century, when the opulent Royal and Splendide hotels overlooking Lake Geneva were built. The famed casino, inspired by the basilica of St. Sophia in Istanbul, was inaugurated in 1912 by architect Jean-Albert Hébrard. Evian became a showplace for spectacular architecture, drawing its inspiration from all over the world, since it catered to a world-class clientele. A whole spectrum of styles—Byzantine and Turkish domes, Greco-Roman columns, neoclassical frescoes, and neo-Gothic turrets—existed alongside one another, accentuated by swirling fin-de-siècle art nouveau patterns.

Royal Hotel, Evian-les-Bains, France.

Evian espoused a form of hydrotherapy that did not exclude other joys of life. After all, the spa had to prove both functional and luxurious in order to match the quality and prestige of its water. "For me, the small town of Evian in the Savoy is full of memories. There in my earliest childhood I had everything, and in adolescence I hoped for everything," wrote poetess Anna de Noailles. She loved the lake, the family house in Amphion, and the artists who came to visit while they were in Evian taking the waters. Marcel Proust was a regular guest at her house. On his first visit to Evian in August 1899, he stayed at the Splendide Hotel, and he returned again and again. His satisfaction with the hotel is evident in a letter he wrote to his mother on September 20, 1899:

> *My dearest mama*
>
> *. . . Lately I've been less than delighted with my health, but it seems to me that sudden changes in the wind and the weather are frequent enough to explain a tendency to breathlessness in the morning and a certain difficulty in sleeping. I'm quite happy to be at the Splendide, for Monsieur Oulif told me that young Weisweiller's asthma was very bad in one of the hotels farther down and that it disappeared as if by magic as soon as he came to the Splendide. . . . A thousand tender kisses.*
>
> *Marcel*

The Royal Hotel was originally built in 1907 for Edward VII, who came to Evian for a fiesta and wanted a hotel built "unlike anything else." The king did not live long enough to see the completion of the Royal, which became one of the great gathering places of international society. Serge Diaghilev, Vaslav Nijinsky, Igor Stravinsky, Pierre Cartier, the Guggenheims, Isadora Duncan, the Duchess of Marlborough, Ida Rubenstein, Greta Garbo, and countless others flocked to the Royal to sit on the Belle Epoque balconies overlooking the lake and take the waters. It was the time of the Rolls-Royce, Hispaño Suiza, and Bugatti. Champagne and caviar, reigning princes and dethroned princes, princes of the arts and letters, princes of business and of the night encountered each other here in a fascinating royal swirl. But it was not until the Queen Mother of England came to stay here in 1983 that the Royal really earned its title. The management went so far as to rent a gilded bed for the royal suite.

The Royal is a beautiful hotel, resembling a sumptuous cruise liner floating on a sea of hills. Surrounding it is a domesticated forest where

Napoleon III tore up the town of Vichy in order to build an enormous spa symbolizing his own imperial image. Ironically, the city slowly rebuilt itself, dwarfing the spa until it was practically nonexistent except for the legend surrounding it. At the turn of the century, it was rebuilt again with neo–Louis XV architecture. During World War II, Vichy became the seat of the Pétain government and the spa was neglected.

The Chomel Springs, Vichy, France.

spotted deer gambol about unafraid. The public room, topped by a dome painted in understated gray and ocher and decorated with the signs of the zodiac and a royal crown and insignia, leads into a series of huge drawing rooms replete with colonnades, vaulted ceilings, domes, and a rotunda. Floral frescoes by Gustave Jaulmes adorn the walls of its restaurant, the Café Royal. A crystal chandelier hangs in the center, illuminating the largest dry floral arrangement I have ever seen. "It is an exquisite jewel box which has to be worthy of the jewels it contains," comments Gilles Janin, the hotel manager.

When I was a guest at the Royal, my room had a balcony facing Lake Geneva, and I spent interminable hours day and night watching the satin-smooth lake and the goings on in the small forest. Spotted white deer (the same kind I later feasted on at the Quellenhof in Bad Ragaz, I'm afraid) grazed in the green expanse of the park. The bucks liked to scratch their backs with their antlers, which were shaped more like elk horns than those of deer. A ferry resembling a sparkling jewel crossed from the northern to the southern shore of the lake frequently at night. Most of the days were hazy that autumn, throwing a veil over the mountains that rise majestically above the lake; the opposite shore displayed bountiful vineyards. One night a few other guests and I sat in a splendid Belle Epoque lounge surrounded by frescoes and listened to two musicians play duets by Boccherini and Spohr as we sipped Evian water—civilized, most civilized—in evening gowns.

During the day I was sprayed with hoses at the Better Living Institute, a stylish fitness and beauty center; I had water continually spritzed on my face for an hour, was wrapped in an algae bath, did water gymnastics, was massaged under a douche, and received hydrotherapy in a giant bathtub—all in Evian mineral water. After taking a nap in an atrium and drinking a gallon of Evian water, I strolled down to Tony's Bar to indulge in a cocktail of all red fruits. It was an unforgettable cocooning experience.

"On stepping aboard Evian's Royal, I have always felt as though I was starting a cruise, motionless, rich in discoveries which bring a feeling of warmth," wrote Jacques Chancel in *Watcher on the Shores.* "Wind, music, that certain something about those around one, and the sky which is not truly blue, all combine to assuage the spirit."

GERMANY

Baden-Baden

The Romans called it Aquae Aureliae; now we know it as Baden-Baden (bath bath). As early as A.D. 117 the Romans were harnessing the radioactive mineral hot springs, which they believed were an elixir capable of curing obesity; rheumatism; arthritis; heart and circulatory problems; metabolic, gynecological, and respiratory disorders; and countless other maladies. Around the springs they built baths with subterranean hot-air systems that still exist. In 213 Emperor Caracalla, a great promoter of spas, decreed that the simple stonework of Caracalla Thermae be embellished with marble and granite.

In the nineteenth century Baden-Baden became the most glamorous watering place on the Continent, and many referred to it as the summer capital of Europe. It was *the* place to see and to be seen in, and the streets teemed with the titled, the wealthy, and the famous. Kings and poets, philosophers, architects, and artists shaped the town's appearance.

In 1808 a gambling bank was established to accommodate wealthy patrons of the casino, which was constructed in 1820 in the right wing of the *Kurhaus* by architect Friedrich Weinbrenner. In 1854 Jacques Benazet furnished this magnificent Belle Epoque edifice in the opulent manner of Versailles, with gilded mirrors and velvet drapes, gold cornices and doors, lavish silk tapestries, and enormous Ming vases. Magnificent crystal chandeliers sparkled above the four gaming rooms, where fashionably dressed gamblers tested their fortune at roulette, baccarat, chemin de fer, and blackjack, and where, until recently, only gold chips were used. Marlene Dietrich called it the most beautiful casino in the world.

The elite promenaded amid Weinbrenner's white columns, and expensive silk gowns rustled as the ladies from the court at St. Petersburg whispered to one another about the Parisian demimondaines. "In Petersburg we don't know how to live. I spent the summer in Baden [*sic*], and you wouldn't believe it," comments a character in Tolstoy's *Anna Karenina*. "I felt quite a young man again. At a glimpse of a pretty woman, my thoughts . . ."

The casino gained a reputation for loose morality; ladies were seen gambling, and gentlemen flaunted their mistresses in public. In 1872, when gambling was banned in Germany, depriving the visitors of their favorite pastime at the watering places, Benazet came up with the clever idea of turning the casino into a private gambling club, and the fun continued.

By 1830 Baden-Baden boasted approximately fifteen thousand visitors a year. Queen Victoria came often because she found the air "so becoming," but later she became disenchanted with the town, agreeing with Empress Augusta of Prussia that Baden-Baden society was so disreputable that "no one can mix in it without loss of character." Napoleon III and later Edward VII continued their patronage, as did Kaiser Wilhelm I, who arrived every summer with twelve horses and twelve coachmen.

Baden-Baden also became a haven for painters, writers, and musicians. Brahms, who initially came to perform, was so taken with the town that he built a villa, which he called his "composing cavern," where he spent every spring and autumn writing music for the next fourteen years. But an even greater attraction for him was the concert pianist Clara Schumann, who lived in Baden-Baden. "My Clara, when I read your words, your eyes seem to look out of them and smile at me," he wrote in a letter. "Dear Clara, you really must make a serious effort to prevent your disconsolate mood from getting the upper hand or becoming permanent. Life is so precious, and that sort of emotional mood is capable of violently destroying one's body. . . . Passions are not a natural part of human beings. They are always exceptions and excesses."

Chopin was often seen in Baden-Baden, and Berlioz came in 1853 to conduct a great music festival. He returned regularly for the next ten years

and there composed his swan song, the opera *Beatrice and Benedict*. Delacroix also spent summers taking the waters and sketching the Oos Valley, where Baden-Baden is nestled. Turgenev wrote in the peace of the valley, as did Dumas fils, Stendhal, Balzac, and George Sand. Fyodor Dostoyevsky and his wife, Anna, spent four years in Baden-Baden and other European spas to satisfy his gambling obsession.

During World War II, Baden-Baden not only was untouched by bombing but also became more exclusive than ever before. Hitler, who was desperate for foreign currency, encouraged the casino's operation, although he himself never visited the town. When the residents discovered that the invading French were planning to attack the spa, they invited them to occupy it peacefully. After the war Baden-Baden became a convalescent center for wounded German officers.

Baden-Baden continues to thrive as an elegant spa, perhaps the most elegant in Europe. I had the privilege of visiting it a few times, a treat indeed, and of staying at the Brenner's Park Hotel, which was built in 1832, a sumptuous palace near the Black Forest, graciously civilized, glowing with the spirit of the past. It is easy to imagine oneself in another time while strolling down an avenue in the adjacent Lichtentaller Allee, a lush, verdant park with a creek gurgling through it. Or walking in the rain, protected by enormous magnolias, catalpas, lindens, ginkoes, and silver maples—some of them more than a century old, digging their octopuslike arms into the earth and sprouting again. Fronting the Allee are century-old villas surrounded by glorious gardens and lawns with dozens of varieties of rhododendrons and azaleas bursting into vivid bloom. A rose garden boasts some 350 classical varieties planted for their beauty and fragrance, the subtle intoxication of which contributes even more to one's sense of well-being. I went from rose to rose, smelling each, reading the names of the people who planted them, and realizing this is what is meant by stopping to smell the roses. I imagined Russian princes driving troikas of white horses down the tree-lined avenues and sensed the ghost of Edward VII wandering among the rose hedges behind the smooth clay tennis courts—Edward had in fact been seen strolling here, dressed as a ghost for a play. I even imagined a criminal lurking behind the dense linden trees, waiting to assassinate a king. I felt transported to the age when Old World royalty came here to enjoy the same kind of pampering I did while taking the waters.

One of the greatest treasures of Baden-Baden undoubtedly is Friedrichsbad, a splendid Roman-Irish bathhouse built in 1869–77 over the ruins of the original Roman baths, where bathing is as much a tradition today as it was two thousand years ago.

The experience of Friedrichsbad resembles a unique treasure hunt that lasts at least two hours and takes you through a maze of rooms opulently appointed with marble floors, painted tiles, cupolas, colonnades, and frescoed walls. It still maintains the *tepidarium, caldarium,* and *frigidarium* of the ancient Roman baths. You follow a prescribed sequence that is inscribed on the wall in each room, specifying how much time you should spend there.

It begins with a leisurely shower, followed by a warm-air bath, then a hot-air bath that makes perspiration flow in healthy torrents, releasing toxins. After another shower to cool off, you are given an invigorating soap-and-brush massage followed by a period of rest on the terra-cotta seats inside a steambath. You then enter a series of thermal pools of varying temperatures, where you can either rest in the water or swim gently and enjoy the solitude, disturbed only by the resounding echo of footsteps and occasional whispers. Then, the treasure: a round, tepid pool under an enormous dome, flooded with light and decorated with the finest marble and statues. This is a place dreams are made of—it is also one where men and women bathe together. (Friedrichsbad has two identical suites of baths designed to segregate the sexes. On certain days, however, mixed bathing is allowed in this central pool and, as is customary in most parts of central and northern Europe, it is done *au naturel.*) If you can tear yourself away from this lovely pool, the following phase is a hot bath with bubbling jets, terminating in a quick dip into a shocking eighteen-degree-Celsius pool. Then you enter a tranquil rotunda with small beds—here the sexes are always separated—where you are wrapped up gently in warm blankets and left to rest or nap.

Feeling deliciously relaxed and revitalized after spending two hours at Friedrichsbad, I strolled through the impeccably landscaped spa park to the Trinkhalle (pump room) to sample the various mineral waters containing manganese, selenium, lithium, iron, and—most intriguing of all, because of

Father Sebastian Kneipp was a nineteenth-century Bavarian monk who preached and practiced hydrotherapy. Based on alternating cold and warm water applications, his treatment included herbal baths, compresses, barefoot walks in dewy grass and snow, exercise, and a mostly vegetarian diet. Father Kneipp is also credited with inventing the herbal wrap, which entails swathing the body in layers of hot, herbally scented towels. Bad Worishofen is now the center of the Kneipp cure, but it has also spread to other parts of the world; there is even a botanical line sold in pharmacies and bath and beauty shops that is wonderful to use in one's own bath at home. The products come in scents such as hops, rosemary, spruce, pine, chamomile, and linden and orange blossom.

its obvious danger and its promise to improve digestion—arsenic. I happened to have digestive problems at the time; after I drank this water, they soon waned. The next day I tried lithium water, after which I felt very happy and giddy. Who knows why—the magic potion or the serenity of this watering place?

Next door to Friedrichsbad is the Caracalla Spa, an ultramodern bathhouse completed in 1985. Its brightly lit entrance hall of blue and white marble, known as the Roman Square, is enhanced by a copy of the Venus of Cnidos, the first known depiction of a bather, created by Praxiteles around 340 B.C. This spa has shops, restaurants, and numerous treatment centers.

Caracalla's ambience is geared more toward fun than sedate relaxation—although sometimes it is difficult to separate the two. Every day half a million gallons of thermal water bubble up from the depths of the Florentine mountain, eventually reaching Caracalla's seven therapeutic pools, two of which are circular outdoor pools adorned by a brimming, mushroom-shaped fountain. During the summer the outdoor pools offer bubbles, massages, and cascades of hot water running over rocks. The interior pools likewise offer myriad attractions, including a pool with jets that has the effect of a giant Jacuzzi, a cool grotto, a large sunken bath, a canal with flowing water, showers for your neck, hot-water spouts, solariums, and an inhalatorium. Caracalla promotes bathing for pleasure—one of the most valuable forms of medicine.

The pleasures of Baden-Baden would be incomplete without the Brenner's Park Hotel, in its luxuriant and peaceful natural setting. Renowned for its superb haute cuisine, impeccable service, and understated elegance, this *grande dame* offers the splendor of the old tradition.

I arrived at Brenner's in midafternoon after a long day's drive and was escorted to a luxurious lounge where afternoon tea was being served to musical accompaniment. A picture window revealed people strolling through the park in the mist. I lost all sense of time.

My suite was palatial and had a balcony overlooking the Lichtentaller Allee and the gurgling creek, the sound of which lulled me to sleep at night.

THE ROMAN IRISH BATH

1 Shower/Body cleansing		5 min.
2 Warm air bath	54 C	15 min.
3 Hot air bath	68 C	5 min.
4 Shower		short
5 Soap and brush massage		8 min.
6 Shower		short
7 Thermal-steam room I	45 C	10 min.
8 Thermal-steam room II	48 C	5 min.
9 Complete thermal bath	36 C	10 min.
10 Thermal jet-spray bath	34 C	15 min.
11 Thermal exercise pool	28 C	5 min.
12 Shower		8 min.
13 Cold-water bath (total submersion)	18 C	short
14 Drying (warm towels)		4 min.
15 Rest period		30 min.
Bathing time incl. rest period	approx.	120 min.

The time indicated for the individual baths is only approximate and can be adjusted in compliance with medical prescription or to suit the needs of the guest.

The bathrooms were utterly inviting, with their Edwardian chrome fixtures, Italian mable floors heated thermostatically from below, and towels warmed on a special rack so that one moves gently into the air after a bath.

Brenner's is a self-contained world; it has its own spa with a spectacular swimming pool surrounded by Pompeian-style frescoed walls, columns, and murals. An enormous picture window beyond the pool overlooks the lush Lichtentaller Allee. The spa houses a Lancaster beauty farm that offers cosmetic and skin-care products and treatments—facials, massage, lymph drainage, and body peeling, to name a few.

Baden-Baden is one of the most romantic places to visit in Europe. In fact, it is a fantastic way to begin a transatlantic trip; taking the waters seems to counteract jet lag and acclimate the traveler quickly to the rhythm of the Continent. After a couple of days of pampering at Brenner's and a long day at Friedrichsbad, the body feels completely rested, the mind cleared, and the spirit restored.

LEFT: *Roman Irish bath at Friedrichsbad, Baden-Baden, Germany.*

RIGHT: *Plan of the Roman Irish Bath at Friedrichsbad, Baden-Baden, Germany, provided to guests when they enter the spa.*

Wiesbaden

"That wholly modern, yet singular city of tranquility and enjoyment of life, out of which you need not venture to see the first green of spring and the trees blossoming. The lilac's sweet scent floats to the farthest lane." That was how Jacob Grimm, one of the famous brothers of the fairy tales, described Wiesbaden, his hometown.

The capital of the state of Hesse, Wiesbaden lies between the vineyards of the Rheingau, which produces fine Riesling wine and champagne, and the forests of the Taunus Mountains. According to legend, its valley was formed when a giant with clumsy, thundering steps fell to the ground with an echoing thud. Being a bad-tempered giant, he took his spear and stabbed the ground in anger. The earth did not like this at all and punished the giant by squirting hot water into his face. The giant became even more enraged and stabbed the earth another twenty-six times, creating the famous hot springs of Wiesbaden.

For more than two thousand years these waters attracted health seekers. Even before the Roman legions established a fortified camp in 12 B.C., the Mattiaci tribe offered sacrifices to the god of the springs. In 55 B.C. Pliny the Elder highly recommended the waters of Aquae Mattiacae to all Roman tourists, and in no time at all, Wiesbaden became a thriving spa town.

During the Middle Ages, as at many other spas, high-spirited visitors used the baths as a pretext to cast decorum aside and pay their erotic respects to the opposite sex. In 1370 a Sorbonne professor visiting his close friend the Abbott of Eberbach expressed consternation at a mural in the abbott's residence depicting "the lasciviousness and lack of inhibitions, and debauched revelling of both clerical and secular men and women."

One remarkable incident in Wiesbaden's history occurred during the Biedermeier period when Dr. Peez, a spa physician, started using the water cures on animals and established a thermal spa for horses. Horses of the wealthy took the waters along with their masters, but apparently not enough of them patronized the equine spa and it soon became extinct.

In 1813 the diplomat and author Johann Isaac von Gerning produced an exuberant eulogy of Wiesbaden:

> *She liberates thousands yet from the monster gout,*
> *From the tentacles crushing his hapless victim*
> *The nymph smiles on the old man, and banishes agony*
> *From the injured warrior, steeling his arm for battle.*

Kaiser-Friedrich-Bad,
Wiesbaden,
Germany.

An English traveler who wrote under the pseudonym "an old man" published a witty account in 1834, entitled *Bubbles from the Brunnens of Nassau:*

> *While creeping around the long corridor of my hotel (Nassauer Hof), I saw one sleepy German after another, whose nightcaps, night-shirts and slippers showed clearly enough that they were headed for the bathroom. A short time later I saw one lady after another dressed in a similar fashion and going precisely in the same direction. Peacefulness, pomp and discretion stood written on their faces and, although I bowed to these undressed people in the usual manner as they passed by, etiquette demands that, in cases such as these, one should refrain from the friendly smile that normally accompanies this sign of reverence, weakening it instead with an expression that is neither too serious nor too solemn.*

He decided to follow these people to the baths.

> *A thick, white, fatty layer of froth precisely of the type normally seen in a pot of broth, covered the surface of the bath and, after a few seconds, I was also lying in it horizontally like my neighbors, allowing the water to soak through. Occasionally I would hear an old man cough, or a young woman sneeze, and in the cell next to mine I could suddenly hear loud splashing coming from the legs of a German woman. . . . Each sigh was audible and whenever a patient liberated himself from the soup, it was possible to hear the blowing and rubbing so clearly as if one were standing next to the person in question.*

Shortly before the end of the nineteenth century, Wiesbaden hoteliers commissioned the following poem for publicity purposes:

> *Who cares for the power of rank and of name?*
> *At Mattium springs we are all just the same.*
> *Who cares for the honor of class and of wealth?*
> *Compared with this fountain of bliss and of health!*

At the turn of the century the Hohenzollerns declared Wiesbaden their summer residence, and members of the Russian imperial family nursed their aches and pains at its thermal springs. The Romanovs left their impression everywhere in Wiesbaden, from the onion-shaped domes of the villas to the graceful Russian Orthodox chapel of Neroberg, where Princess Elizaveta Mikhailovna—the wife of Prince Adolf, the last Duke of Nassau, and a niece of Czar Nicholas—is buried.

I took a small mountain railway, the Nerobergbahn, which runs entirely on water, up to Neroberg, with its breathtaking panorama of the entire city. It was a clear day and I had a splendid view of the Rheingau's sprawling vineyards. I was surrounded by beech forests rustling in the wind, but it must have taken more than the rustling trees to lure the European aristocracy to Wiesbaden—namely, the rustling of exquisite silk gowns at the glittering parties and sumptuous game tables.

The casino in Wiesbaden is one of the oldest in the world, having a gambling concession as early as 1771. In 1810, when a gaming room was provided in the *Kurhaus,* the cultural center suddenly became the roulette tables. Roulette was the magic word: in the White Room the stakes were gold; in the Red Room wagers were in talers; and smaller bets were placed at the so-called Communal Table. Fyodor Dostoyevsky gambled away his last ruble here in 1871—he lost three thousand rubles at the casino in short order—and departed forever, leaving behind an unpaid hotel bill and a copy of his novel *The Gambler,* which he had written there—in the book he called it "Roulettenburg"—five years earlier.

This unpaid bill is the historical focal point of the Hotel Nassauer Hof. This hotel is the delight of Wiesbaden, a grand hotel with a thermal spring bubbling underneath it. When the spring was discovered by the Romans in A.D. 83, their autocratic Emperor Domitian ordered a stone fortress built where the hotel now stands. This military base was withdrawn under Hadrian in 122 and the fort was converted into a thermal spa. Centuries later the first recorded mention of Wisibada (which in time became Wiesbaden) speaks of an inn at this location, where the royal messengers to France changed horses. This building was damaged by fires during the sixteenth and seventeenth centuries, and another inn and baths were built on the site.

In 1903 the Nassauer Hof became the gallery of Europe for a glittering public who came to observe the meeting between Kaiser Wilhelm II and Czar Nicholas II. Among the leading courtiers of the two emperors who stayed and dined at the hotel, conversation focused on the desirability of German backing in the impending Russo-Japanese War.

When Europe was engulfed by World War I, the Nassauer Hof was converted into a military hospital, the housekeeper and staff acting as auxiliary nurses. During the Nazi era Hitler often visited Wiesbaden, and Heinrich Himmler actually stayed at the Nassauer Hof, even sending flowers to two Jewish women guests. During the night air raids of February and March 1945, the Nassauer Hof burned to the ground again and lost many of its valuable documents. In 1968 the Stinnes Company invested twenty million marks to raise the hotel from its ashes and restore its past grandeur.

It is a gracious hotel, immediately infusing a sense of ease and intimacy. It has a fine spa on the fifth floor, with windows all around, offering a gorgeous view of Wiesbaden. Its magnificent thermal swimming pool is fed directly from the Kochbrunnenquelle hot spring under the building, which, registering 67 degrees Celsius, flows at the rate of forty liters a minute. Since this temperature is too hot to bathe in, it is cooled down naturally to a comfortable 32 degrees.

The spa houses a Lancaster beauty farm, a franchise that offers full beauty treatments and graces other fine hotels, including Brenner's Park in Baden-Baden and the Kempinski in Frankfurt. The complex also has two Finnish saunas with plunge pools and a Japanese garden of rocks, bamboo, and Japanese maple, reminding us once more that we live in many worlds.

Wiesbaden is a unique city that seems to know how to give expression to the joy of living while preserving its idyllic character. It lives, as Jacob Grimm put it, "in the center of the world's pulsing, living heart."

BELGIUM

Spa

The word *spa* may come from the Walloon *espa* (fountain). It may also have its origin in the Latin word *spargere,* "to scatter, sprinkle, moisten," or may be an acronym of the latin phrase *sanitas per aquas.* The name was first adopted by this famed resort, founded in 1326, in the wooded hills of the Ardennes of Belgium, near Liège. However, the word did not come into common use until Emperor Charles IV discovered the great Bohemian spa at Carlsbad.

In the center of the town of Spa stands the Pouhon Pierre-le-Grand. The Walloon word *pouhon* (spring) derives from the old French *puison,* a place where water is drawn, or from *poison,* which derives from the Latin *potio,* meaning "potion" or "drink."

Coins bearing the likeness of Emperor Nerva (who ruled A.D. 96–98) were excavated near the Pouhon Pierre-le-Grand, an indication that Spa was also established by the Romans. It is said that Pliny the Elder, the celebrated Roman naturalist who lived during the first century A.D., was alluding to Spa when he described a mysterious fountain in which bubbles sparkle.

Poster for the Exposition des Sports, Spa, Belgium, 1904.

During the Dark Ages the Spa springs figured in a veritable cult centered around St. Remaclus, who was both bishop and apostle of the untamed Ardennes. A mighty builder of monasteries and a destroyer of idols, he reputedly possessed powers to purify fountains and generate springs. Despite the difficulties of travel in those days, people came from afar to obtain relief from their ailments by taking the waters of the springs. Often the healing was miraculous. The early manuscript *Miracula S. Remacli* (851–861) relates the story of a blind woman who bathed her eyes in the Spa waters and regained her sight immediately.

The legend of St. Remaclus continued to live on in people's consciousness. At the end of the Middle Ages, bridegrooms took their brides to drink the waters of Spa's Sauvenière spring because it enjoyed a reputation for imparting fertility. An imprint of St. Remaclus's foot was reputedly left on a stone; if a young woman placed her foot in this imprint and drank some of the magical waters, she was assured of progeny. This legendary footprint was rediscovered during a recent excavation.

In the Middle Ages the commercial possibilities of Spa's miraculous waters began to be exploited. By 1351 the town was so flooded with visitors that a cure tax had to be imposed. But the real influx of foreign visitors began in the sixteenth century, including such illustrious personalities as Margaret of Navarre, Henry III of France, and Montaigne. Henry VIII's court physician was credited as being the first to use the waters of Spa to treat rheumatism. Other monarchs and statesmen added to Spa's glamour over the years: Queen Christina of Sweden, Russia's Peter the Great, a fugitive Charles II of England, Disraeli, and the Austrian emperor Joseph II, who called Spa the café of Europe. Mark Twain, Freud, Gogol, and Nietzsche sublimated their skepticism under the influence of Spa's sparkling thermal waters. Casanova, who flaunted his concupiscence through the watering holes of Europe, was especially seduced by Spa. In his diaries he noted that he was most fortunate to find the last available room in town—a cluttered, windowless dive shared by others.

In the hall at Pouhon Pierre-le-Grand is a composite mural by Antoine Fontaine representing an impressive array of visitors, from Pliny the Elder and St. Remaclus to Victor Hugo, Adelina Patti, Margaret of Valois, and Cosimo de' Medici. You discover that Dumas fils stayed at Hôtel les Bains, and the composer Spontini in a house on rue du Marche. The French composer Meyerbeer used to ride a donkey along the Avenue of Trees and the duchesse d'Orléans transported herself by camel. History itself is etched in the gaming table, where people came to play faro, craps, or trente et quarante.

Because of these impressive patrons, Spa water was hailed as the "Queen of the Waters." Its curative qualities induced Kaiser Wilhelm II to establish his main headquarters in Spa in 1918. He himself lived at Neubois castle, where people are still amazed at the concrete bomb shelter constructed for his safety.

Today Spa is a small Belgian town nestled in the pine-covered Ardennes hills. Most of the fine old hotels have been turned into sanatoriums with faceless modern embellishments, but if we look closely, we can still see the past reflected in its waters.

ITALY

The Italians consider mineral water an everyday necessity; meals are always accompanied by a bottle of mineral water and a bottle of wine. These two beverages are never served separately. In Roman times slaves were trained to dilute wine with water so it was just right.

Italians take the curative powers of the waters seriously, considering them as valid as any pharmaceutical medicine, if not more so, because of their historical import. Hot springs are so valuable to the Italians that the government owns them and merely grants concessions to the bottling companies. And the *terme,* the thermal spring resort, is considered so essential for one's well-being that the cures are paid for by the state medical system. It is a pleasant way, especially for older people, to enjoy a paid-for vacation.

Montecatini Terme

Anyone who has seen Nikita Mikhalkov's *Dark Eyes* cannot forget the image of the lovesick Marcello Mastroianni wading through a pool of *fango* (black lava and yellow sulfur mud) like some ridiculous primordial creature. *Dark Eyes* is not Mastroianni's first film set in the stylish Tuscan spa of Montecatini Terme. He was there once before for the filming of Fellini's epic farce *8½,* whose famous arrival scene was shot at the marble-and-bronze train station just on the outskirts of town.

Montecatini offers a certain cinematic elegance, making it an ideal location for filmmakers. When I was there, I had just missed Faye Dunaway and Klaus Maria Brandauer, who had been there to film Stefan Zweig's *The Burning Secret*—even though the story itself is set in the Austrian spa at Semmering. It is about a beautiful woman who brings her fragile adolescent son to take the waters. She falls victim to a decadent Austrian baron who courts the boy in order to seduce his mother—a typical spa romance.

Montecatini was also discovered during Roman times. Since then, many of Europe's royal families and greatest artists have ceremoniously sprawled in its *fango* baths and consumed gallons of its saline waters in pursuit of a cure for the perils of overindulging in the good life.

Its graceful architectural style, gardens, and statues epitomize the Belle Epoque; since the late nineteenth century, it has been considered the most elegant spa in Italy. The waters of its five springs—Tamerici, Torretta, Regina, Tettucio, and Rinfresco—reputedly help cure liver maladies, digestive disorders, tropical illnesses, gynecological problems, and obesity.

In the basement of some of the establishments, special machines resembling cement mixers constantly churn out the concoction of dark volcanic mud and mineral water known as *fango.* I was told that it takes at least six months of mixing to reach the right consistency. In various tubs and pools, visitors immerse themselves in *fango,* which supposedly draws toxins out of the pores and cures arthritic pains. There is something wonderful about being buried under the mud—a special way to hide.

I stayed at the Grand Hotel e La Pace, the setting for *Dark Eyes,* which has housed Mary Pickford and Douglas Fairbanks, Sr., Clark Gable, Grace Kelly, Katharine Hepburn, Toscanini, von Karajan, the Kennedys, and the Duke and Duchess of Windsor. The Grand Hotel was built in 1870 and later merged with La Pace Hotel. It has also been the haunt of many great composers and singers, including Puccini, Richard Strauss, Caruso, and Leoncavallo. Leoncavallo died in Montecatini in August 1919. Christian Dior also died there while trying to lose weight. The hotel is a neo-Renaissance palazzo painted Milano yellow, the predominant villa color, and is set in a park in the center of town.

When people arrive in Montecatini, they are examined by a physician who prescribes the most suitable treatment and assigns them to one of the Montecatini water establishments. Tettucio, which has become the pump room for tasting all the Montecatini waters, stays open from May to October; during this time three hundred thousand people come to take the waters. The other establishments, including Leopoldine, Tamerici, and Excelsior, offer various forms of hydrotherapy.

Tettucio is always very lively. Every morning some thirteen thousand people pass through a thirteen-hundred-year-old gate leading to the portico of the establishment to drink the waters from one of the five sources. Afterward they go for a stroll in the park, because walking is part of the cure.

Tettucio was established in the seventeenth century. In 1925 it was refurbished as a neo-Renaissance temple with dramatic domes, arches, fountains, and painted ceramic tiles representing different stages of a person's life: L'Infanzia, L'Adolescenza, La Bellezza, La Forza, La Maturità, La Vecchiaia, and so on. The heron and the frog, symbols of Montecatini, appear everywhere—even the local political party is called the Heron—becoming part of the iconography of the fountains, reliefs, and wall detail. Sala Portoghesi, built by architect Paolo Portoghesi, is the most recent addition to Tettucio. A modern realization of Gothic forms, it has wooden columns that resemble an intricate forest and have the perfect symmetry of a cathedral.

Since the Montecatini waters are good for most gastrointestinal ailments and have a purgative effect, Tettucio is equipped with three thousand meticulously maintained bathrooms that are constantly in use. People walk around carrying special drinking glasses engraved with the words "Montecatini Terme," as an orchestra plays in the background, accompanied by a lovely voice singing arias. The music contributes greatly to the stylish surreal quality of the architecture.

None of the Montecatini spring waters are table variety, but there is a belief that drinking unappetizing water escalates the healing process. Toting around my own drinking glass marked off like a measuring cup, I drank the Tettucio water, which was steaming hot, acrid, excessively salty, and pungent. Yet I was told that Tettucio is the mildest of the Montecatini springs, and that one has to work up to the others. I recalled some entries from Montaigne's journal, written during the summer of 1581 while he was traveling through these same thermal towns of Italy: "the water of Tettucio, which I tasted; it is salty. I have some suspicion that the apothecaries, instead of sending to get it near Pistoia, where they say it is, sophisticate

ABOVE LEFT: *Sala Portoghesi, Tettucio establishment, Montecatini Terme, Italy.*

ABOVE RIGHT: *Toretta fountain in the Tettucio establishment, Montecatini Terme, Italy.*

LEFT: *Entrance of the Tettucio establishment, Montecatini Terme, Italy.*

some natural water; for I found its taste extraordinary, besides the saltiness. . . . They consider sweating virtually fatal, and also sleeping after drinking." It is fascinating how little the beliefs and customs of taking the waters have changed over the centuries. To this day people stroll in the park after taking the waters, to avoid falling asleep.

Façade of the Berzieri Baths, Salsomaggiore, Italy.

The second day of my visit I took the chance of tasting Tamerici water and found the minerals overpowering; it was time to stop.

Princess Marcella Borghese's Montecatini Terme cosmetics and skin products are sold in Tettucio; their advertisements are designed to perpetuate the legend of this romantic spa. I had used their *fango* in a tube long before I went to Montecatini. I was astonished to discover that the products were not actually produced in Montecatini Terme but in the United States.

Like most of modern Italy, Montecatini is a combination of the elegant and the shabby. But the center of town has resisted modern afflictions, and a stroll through Viale Verdi, a beautifully landscaped walk with stone steps and colonnades, toward the spa buildings, as the music of Verdi or Puccini wafts through the air, is a transporting experience.

Salsomaggiore

Salsomaggiore is a *terme* in northern Emilia-Romagna, where the foothills of the Apennines meet the Lombard plain. The Romans favored it primarily for the curative powers of its iodine spring waters, which were also a rich source of cooking salt. The benefits of the spring were rediscovered in 1839 when a doctor named Lorenzo Berzieri treated a young girl suffering from osteitis with iodine water and she recovered instantly.

The Berzieri bathhouse in Salsomaggiore has by far the most ornate and flamboyant spa architecture I have ever seen. Although construction started before World War I, it was inaugurated in 1923 and gained a reputation as the most beautiful baths in the world.

On the building façade, framed by two vicious-looking chimeras in heraldic poses, is an inscription that reads, "A temple of health, not dedicated to leisure connected with healing, but to healing itself"—a motto that seems to contradict the opulence of this pleasure dome. Built in an excessive art deco style with Orientalist allusions—a Chinese bestiary, tiles resembling an Oriental carpet, and Mesopotamian architecture—it could serve beautifully as a set for Verdi's *Aida*. A journalist I know calls it "a hyperbole in Parma-Babylonian style." Its seductive ambience seems designed more to stimulate carnal impulses than to promote spiritual healing—a foreshadowing of the changes to come in the social style of spas.

Salsomaggiore is the favored retreat of the stylish Milanese, who inevitably stay at the exclusive Hotel Milanese. Over the years the spa has attracted such luminaries as Verdi, Marie Louise of Austria (second wife of Napoleon), and Sophia Loren, but it does not quite share the intensity of Montecatini.

San Pellegrino

San Pellegrino lies along the Brambana River in a verdant valley in Lombardy that receives abundant rain all year round. The small roads winding through the surrounding hills are dotted with attractive villas set amid lush greenery. San Pellegrino's springs have been known since Roman times and were rediscovered in the twelfth century. Leonardo da Vinci was among the illustrious pilgrims—*pellegrino* means "pilgrim"—who came to take their waters.

The spa facilities in San Pellegrino were established in 1848, and the bottling operation began in 1899. In its natural form the water is uncarbonated and has a slight mineral taste. Carbonation is later added in the nearby bottling plant.

The cure center still has most of the original tubs and circular Scottish showers that were popular during the early part of this century. In the basement, *fango* is always churning. The pump room on the hillside above is paved with marble and adorned with neoclassical murals. Nearby is the casino, an art nouveau extravaganza built at the turn of the century by the architect Romolo Squadrelli. Its imposing but elegant façade is rich in decorative stuccowork, bas-reliefs, and trompe-l'oeil paintings imitating various natural marbles and granite. A bright entrance hall supported by eight Verona marble columns leads into an impressive stairway crowned with a stained-glass skylight portraying the twelve signs of the zodiac. The walls of the stairwell are decorated with opulent frescoes depicting beautiful allegorical figures; the virtues they represent, such as truth and solidarity, are inscribed in Latin. Busts of the composers Wagner, Beethoven, and Donizetti, placed on pedestals, lend an operatic quality to the ambience.

The *salone della festa,* or gambling room, is the most solemn part of the casino, in contrast to those in Baden-Baden and Evian: presumably, money cannot be gambled in a giddy and distracting environment. However, gambling has not been permitted in the casino since 1946, and the building now belongs to the municipality, which rents it out for weddings and fashion shows. There is talk in the parliament of reopening it as a casino, but the Italians say it will never happen.

This is the casino that Fellini used as a setting for *Juliet of the Spirits,* in which, as in *8½, La Dolce Vita, The Nights of Cabiria, La Strada,* and *Satyricon,* his recurrent obsession with water is reflected.

Across the river from the casino is an enormous edifice bearing the inviting sign GRAND HOTEL. Built in 1904, also by Squadrelli, it is now completely boarded up and strangled with overgrown vegetation. A few years ago it was estimated that restoration of the building alone, not including interiors, would cost about $20 million. So there it sits in the heart of town, neglected, making us wish that it could somehow come back to life and revive the bygone era of romantic spas and grand hotels.

Saturnia

Miles of thermal streams, waterfalls, and limestone-carved pools stretch throughout Tuscany. One of its unique watering places is the sulfurous stream of Saturnia, which is heated by a volcano. For miles, you can see people submerged in its waters or bracing themselves against the force of its waterfalls. I was told that people return here at night and bathe naked in the moonlit pools, steam rising from their bodies while the sound of the gently rumbling falls enters their dreams. Nearby there is a civilized establishment, Terme di Saturnia, with a hotel, pool, and various sorts of hydrotherapy. The water may be the same but the ambience is radically different; here, visitors have access to the amenities of civilization and are further removed from nature.

Driving through the fertile Tuscan hills, I saw distant pockets of steam rising above the wheat fields, vineyards, and forests. I stopped and asked some peasants what this smoke was. The answer, of course, was "terme." This is what people must have meant in the Middle Ages when they talked about the mountains smoking in winter.

SWITZERLAND

Bad Ragaz

According to legend, the healing waters of Bad Ragaz were first discovered by a thirteenth-century knight on a hunting expedition. Located in eastern Switzerland, in the foothills of the Alps near Liechtenstein, Bad Ragaz is fed by three thermal springs originating in the Tamina gorge three miles away.

ABOVE: *Thermal cascades, Saturnia, Italy.*

LEFT: *Fountains at San Pellegrino, Italy.*

The gorge is a geological wonder; water gushes inside a cathedrallike cave with a crack in its ceiling, through which diffused light is filtered. The eerie light, the rumbling sound of the streams, and the mist generated by the thermal water all conspire to create the unworldly sensation of being inside a tropical cathedral during an earthquake.

Pfäffers, the ancient baths located at the bottom of the gorge, is described by Augustin Stöcklin in *Historia de Fabariensibus Thermis naturaliter caldis* (1630) as "a horrible site of deepest solitude, similar to the Acheron or the Stygian swamps." Indeed, in the Middle Ages the access to the spa was terrifying: visitors could get down to the gorge only by means of hanging ladders or ropes, and it was so crowded in the baths that no one could even move. "There they sat in the dark like souls in Saint Patrick's purgatory," wrote Sebastian Münster in *Cosmographia* (1550). Nevertheless, it became a meetingplace of the humanists, and Paracelsus, the celebrated naturalist, physician, and philosopher, lived here in 1535. By 1839, the spring waters were being channeled from Pfäffers through a wooden pipeline into the valley of Ragaz, where they became easily accessible.

Bad Ragaz is another of the spas that became fashionable in the nineteenth century and continues to attract an impressive clientele. The Hungarian-born conductor George Szell, for instance, could not function without regenerating his system here. The grand hotel Quellenhof, built in 1869 by architect Bernhard Simon, was closed during World War II but reopened in 1957 after a complete renovation. It is a fairyland of a place, set in a carefully maintained park with a breathtaking view of the Alps. It has its own thermal pool and spa facilities.

I arrived at Quellenhof one evening in the middle of autumn and found myself sitting in a cozily lit Alpine restaurant, warmed by a blazing fire and filled with a sense of being close to nature. The hunters had delivered their bounty, and we were offered a seven-course meal featuring a wondrous variety of game: hare pâté, wild pig, magnificent venison, and fowl whose names I do not know. Despite my vegetarian preferences, I appreciated the meat; it somehow felt correct eating the flesh of animals with which the local population has always lived in ecological harmony. As it turned out, this evening was a celebration marking the start of a new hunting season, a tradition dating back to pagan days. Later our host told me that each hunter had to be over fifty years old, was allowed only one deer a season, and was required to go up into the mountains and feed an animal in winter.

Hotel Quellenhof,
Bad Ragaz,
Switzerland, 1880,
lithograph.

Artist unknown,
Pfäffers Bath in the
Fourteenth Cen-
tury, *1750, oil on
canvas, 21⅞ x 15⅞ in.
(55 x 40 cm).
Thermalbäder- und
Grand Hotels AG*

*Poster, Baden,
Switzerland.*

Baden, Switzerland.

Thermal Pool,
Verenahof Hotel,
Baden, Switzerland.

Baden

Baden, or Aquae Helveticae, is a picturesque medieval spa on the Limmat River near Zurich. According to legend, it was first discovered in 58 B.C. by a young man named Sigawyn, who found his missing goat perched on a rock out of which hot water was gushing. Baden's reputation as a watering hole goes back more than two thousand years to the time when those intrepid bath builders, the Romans, used their skills to harness its rich mineral waters for their bathing pleasure. Initially the site of the hot springs was a large soldier camp. During the Middle Ages the Hapsburgs adopted Baden as their home base and the spa served as a haven where wealthy bathers wined and dined on floating trays. When the first railway line was built between Baden and Zurich in the mid-nineteenth century, easier access attracted large crowds to the spa. People arrived with their servants, furniture, and countless other possessions and stayed for weeks, sometimes months. Young married women came alone and sat in the hot waters for long periods of time until they developed "bath rash," which was very fashionable. Famous guests at Baden included the swiss painter Arnold Böcklin, Oskar Kokoschka, Richard Strauss, and Count Zeppelin. Hermann Hesse was a frequent guest for twenty years and wrote many of his books here. His novel *Kurgast* is full of anecdotes about the place.

Baden's mineral-rich thermal waters are buried nearly a mile deep in the earth, where they lay hidden for twenty to thirty thousand years before bubbling forth as nineteen springs that yield a quarter of a million gallons of water a day.

The spa quarter of Baden consists of a central square, the Kurplatz, surrounded by a cluster of colorful old hotels. The entire scene resembles a Hollywood set that might at any minute be struck, leaving nothing but façades. But in fact, there is a great deal more here than mere façades. Each of these hotels, although much smaller than those in other spas I have mentioned, has its own establishment specializing in an assortment of water cures and other treatments. Here, as in France and Italy, government-issued prescriptions make it possible for people to sit on terraces overlooking the hypnotic Limmat River and be pampered. Impressive fountains in the Kurplatz invite you to taste the waters, which are hot and profusely sulfurous. A short stroll leads to a casino, which was once a lovely Belle Epoque building but has recently been replaced by a modern structure of no particular distinction.

Outside the Limmathof Hotel, near the river, is an enormous outdoor thermal pool. When you are bathing in it, the mist rises all around you and you see the world as if through a silk stocking. Even on snowy winter days people wade in the pool, moving from one jet to another, each jet directed to stimulate a different part of the anatomy. Baden is still a solid spa where guests take the waters seriously.

CZECHOSLOVAKIA

Marienbad

Forty thousand people frequent spas in Czechoslovakia every year. Although most Czech and other Eastern European spas resemble the one depicted in Milan Kundera's *The Farewell Party,* that kind of communist asceticism has not succeeded in suppressing nostalgia for the opulence of Marienbad (Marianske Lazne in Czech) in Bohemia, with its sculptural wrought-iron colonnade where crowds once strolled while taking the waters. In spite of its title, Alain Resnais's avant-garde film *Last Year at Marienbad* was not filmed at Marienbad but at the spa of Nymphenburg in Ba-

Last Year at Mar-
ienbad, *1962.*
Copyright New
Yorker Films.

Werner Weiskönig,
Marienbad, *1937,*
color lithograph, 50 x
35⅜ in. (127 x 90
cm). Poster collection,
Museum für Ge-
staltung, Zurich

varia. The endless labyrinth of corridors and finely manicured gardens in Resnais's film are a far cry from the ambience of the real town of Marienbad, which is mostly neobaroque in style, with villas and hotels that once sparkled with glamour and whose exteriors are encrusted with stucco sculptures of spa iconography. Caryatids and angels are everywhere, especially on the façade of the old casino.

Colonnade, Marienbad (Marianske Lazne), Czechoslovakia.

Marienbad was among the most desirable and elegant spas in the nineteenth century and, like most other fashionable spas at the time, became an emporium of extramarital affairs. Many of the respectable ladies who graced Marienbad and Carlsbad had seasonal admirers who were known as "bath shadows." Goethe was seventy-four years old when he took the waters of Marienbad, but his real cure probably came from courting a nineteen-year-old girl. It was also at Marienbad that Wagner surrendered himself to the water nymphs who inspired him to compose *Lohengrin.*

When the spa fell into the hands of the communist government, it took on the air of a sanatorium with sterile-looking rooms and linoleum floors. But since the overturn of communism in Czechoslovakia, there has been a concerted effort to restore Marienbad to its former glory.

Spa Revival

Spas fell out of favor between the two world wars. The pace of life had become faster, the fight for survival more aggressive, and the work ethic more intense. The upper class lost its status as the leisure class, and members of the new affluent class were partial to taking package tours to their favorite seaside towns. They also preferred the privacy and security of resorts with gates and guards. The days of dangerous liaisons at the spas were over.

But since the 1980s, spa culture has been undergoing a revival, as a result of people's concern over environmental hazards. Shrewd entrepreneurs have seized upon the renewed interest in spas and combined the appeal of taking the waters with every possible fitness craze, from aerobics to cell implantation. The glamorous social life of the nineteenth-century spas may never be duplicated, but it has been replaced successfully by luxurious hedonism. We have thus come full circle since the Romans established their *thermae.*

Some attribute the initial success of Mikhail Gorbachev's political career to his former position as party leader of Stavropol in the Caucasus, a region famous for its spas. Not only did this area get funding to upgrade its spas, but also it was frequented by high-ranking party officials, such as Yuri Andropov and Aleksei Kosygin, who came to take the waters and became captivated by Gorbachev's charisma. At the beginning of his presidency, Gorbachev encouraged Soviets to cut down on vodka consumption and increase their intake of mineral waters.

Spa in the true sense implies a balancing of mind and spirit through interaction with water, but today it is a very loosely generalized word, meaning anything from fiberglass Jacuzzis to beauty parlors at department stores, to a room with a couple of rusty weight machines and possibly a sauna in a chain hotel, to fitness resorts, to refuges near hot springs.

The spa business is bursting with innovative programs in the nineties. For example, the Norwegian cruise ship *Norway* now offers "ancient Rome" on its Caribbean cruise—a six-thousand-square-foot full-service spa, as opulent as any on land. It features a complete package of therapeutic water, mineral, plant, and herb treatments. The advertisement for it reads: "You not only get a spa vacation, you get an incomparable cruise experience." How can one top that?

I firmly believe that there is more to a thermal spring than heat, and that warm waters are conducive to more than plant growth. They are ideal for human evolution, for what Teilhard de Chardin called "the metamorphosis of man." It is significant that some of the most significant consciousness raising centers in America are located at hot springs. It may well be that water extracts a subtle energy from deep within the earth and transmits it to truthseekers. Or perhaps the relaxation of the body while immersed in soothing warm water creates a new and enlightened ecology of the mind, allowing quantum leaps in understanding.

BILL KEYSING, *Great Hot Springs of the West* (1984)

American Spas

Many moons before the arrival of the Puritans, Native Americans from the Atlantic to the Pacific had put their faith in the rejuvenative powers of the waters. They regarded hot springs as effective medicine and chose them as sites of tribal councils, holy rites, and healing centers. The ancient Paiute Indian healing grounds, for example, built around the Pah Tempe hot springs in southwestern Utah, were recently resanctified by a local medicine man.

Some tribes extolled the virtues of lying spread-eagle in the waters; others believed in drinking them in great quantities. According to legend, an intertribal rule specified, "No fighting at a hot spring." Since warring tribes gathered in these places to bathe their wounds, hot springs became sanctuaries of peace.

Early European settlers in the New World who remembered the joys of the spas back home did not have to recross the ocean to take the Old World waters. By observing Native Americans, they became aware of an abundance of hot springs and special cures their new land had to offer.

The Assiniboin Indians of western Canada believed in the rejuvenative powers of the springs in Bow Valley; in time, wealthy white people flocked to these waters in the hopes of restoring their youth. The Seneca of western New York used the natural oil floating on the springs in their territory to treat rheumatism. When Gen. Benjamin Lincoln was leading his Revolu-

Edward Curtis, Before the White Man Came, 1924, photograph.

tionary troops through western Pennsylvania, he allowed the men to stop at a spring covered with oil to bathe their aching joints, which were immediately freed from pain. They also took advantage of the spring water, which functioned as a gentle purgative. Later, French Lick Springs in Indiana became a mecca for the obese and the constipated, its so-called Pluto water being a natural and powerful laxative. An advertisement for Poland Spring in Maine claimed that its water "Cures Dyspepsia! Cures Liver Complaints of Long Standing! Cures Gravel! Drives out all Tumors and Purifies the Blood." And the waters of Hot Springs, Arkansas, allegedly cured sufferers of almost everything, from syphilis to melancholy.

Transcendental tourism spread rapidly through America. Ailing citizens traveled hundreds of miles by stagecoach in order to soak in their favorite hot springs. Like their European counterparts, some of these watering holes became successful resorts where the rich and famous mingled. Saratoga Springs in New York, Poland Spring in Maine, Hot Springs in Arkansas, Boyes Hot Springs in California, and many other sources developed into elegant spas. Originally, several separate bathhouses were built so that the more puritanical visitors could bathe indoors, in private. By the end of the nineteenth century, however, these spas had shed their chaste image, adapting all the trappings of late Victorian society and becoming as permissive as their European predecessors.

"The beautiful ladies, and those who would be beautiful, come to the waters of Hot Springs," proclaimed a guidebook in the 1880s. "Those who have ruined their complexion by excessive use of cosmetics will renew beauty and youth and regain soft, fair, and clear complexions. Those who feel the heavy hand of time being placed upon them, and their looking glass reveals wrinkles and mole patches, can by bathing in and drinking these waters so improve their complexion as to appear several years younger than their actual age."

People went to the spas seeking to soothe body and soul, and most came away fulfilled. It did not matter whether the spas were actually responsible for this healing. Detaching oneself from the stress of everyday living was the first step toward recovery.

The spas claimed to offer healthy foods. Mark Twain once said, "The only way to keep your health is to eat what you don't want, drink what you don't like, and do what you'd rather not." But the cuisine that was considered healthy in those days was very different from what we consider healthy today. It included dishes high in calories, fat, and cholesterol, ranging from lobster Newburg and pickled lamb's tongue to butter cake and cream puffs. To eat well meant to eat a lot; it was considered healthy to be a bit plump.

Hot-spring resorts were almost always situated in the countryside, and city people loved getting away from it all under the pretext of taking the waters. But around the turn of the twentieth century, fashions changed, favoring the city, and the countryside suddenly lost its allure. The spas suffered severe financial losses and slowly began to disintegrate.

During the 1920s and 1930s they attempted to attract visitors by offering entertainment. Many of them built speakeasies and dance halls. In the 1940s and 1950s, however, the popularity of the spas reached an all-time

Foot bath in the mineral springs of Arrowhead Springs, California, 1926.

low. The war was one reason, of course, but also other types of recreation spots—seaside and lakeside resorts, for example—were drawing vacationers away from spas. Moreover, the therapeutic reputation of mineral waters was largely eclipsed by the mass production of artificial healing agents. So the dance halls, bathhouses, and grand hotels of the spas began to go to seed, and many hot springs were soon forgotten, except by the locals, and for the most part remained so until the 1960s, when health enthusiasts, environmentalists, and spiritual visionaries once again rediscovered the magic of hot springs.

Spas are now experiencing a great revival all over the world, and America is taking the lead. Unlike their European counterparts, however, many of the new American spas do not revolve exclusively around water, although they continue to use water in various therapeutic ways. In landscaping, for example, man-made forms of water—ponds, waterfalls, and fountains—are designed to appeal to the senses and bring harmony to the soul. Hydrotherapy is still common, as are algae and *fango* therapies, and some spas have been experimenting with thalassotherapy, which uses seawater instead of spring water. All serve and encourage guests to drink large quantities of mineral water from other famous springs. In California, for example, Golden Door serves Evian; Cal-a-Vie offers Vittel. We no longer have to travel to the sources of these waters; they come to us in bottles.

I look for hot springs wherever I go. In the process I have come across myriad watering places, ranging from Zen monasteries like Tassajara and enlightenment centers like Esalen to bubbling holes in the mud in Calistoga—all in California—to legendary five-star hotels like Greenbrier in West Virginia. No matter what the surroundings are, a mysterious peace always descends upon me whenever I enter the magic waters.

Traditional Spas

H. B. Settle, Taking the Waters at Congress Spring in Congress Park, Saratoga Springs, N.Y., *1915. The George S. Bolster Collection of the Historical Society of Saratoga Springs, N.Y.*

Saratoga Springs

Saratoga Springs in New York, Hot Springs in Arkansas, Safety Harbor in Florida, and White Sulphur Springs in West Virginia are among the few American hot springs that have managed to weather the storms of time. Saratoga represents perhaps the ultimate grandeur in American spa culture. Believed to be a primeval fountain, Saratoga's underground spring was discovered by the Iroquois centuries ago. The Iroquois believed that the spring had special healing powers and kept its location a secret until 1767. Once the secret was out, however, the spring began attracting such noteworthy visitors as George Washington and Alexander Hamilton, and bottlers started fighting over rights to its waters until they were declared to be in the public domain. Saratoga boasted two kinds of water—a slightly saline water that acted as a laxative, and an alkaline water that helped digestion.

The village of Saratoga Springs, established in 1826, was probably the closest thing in America to a European spa town, but with its own special flair. The predominant architectural style of the villas that still line Union Avenue, for example, is Victorian rather than Belle Epoque, and they are built of wood instead of marble. During the Gay Nineties, "sipper" boys ladled water into monogrammed cups for the likes of Lillian Russell and her beau, Diamond Jim Brady. Presidents, famous athletes, gangsters, and showgirls came to play in this stylish water town.

In the nineteenth century gambling and horse racing flourished in Saratoga. Since gambling no longer exists, the casino has become a museum, but racing has remained an important part of the town's social scene. In the 1930s more than a hundred and fifty thousand people came to Saratoga annually to bet on the horses and enjoy the salubrious climate while soaking in and sipping the waters. The Union dining room at the Grand Union Hotel regularly served a thousand guests at a time. In 1935 a new spa complex was opened, helped by a federal grant of $8.5 million authorized by Franklin D. Roosevelt, who also sponsored the building of a two-thousand-acre state park encompassing the springs and the neo-colonial Gideon Putnam Hotel, projects reflecting the energy of the WPA.

A great deal of effort has gone into restoring Saratoga Springs to its old grandeur. Although the Grand Union and Grand Central hotels have burned down, the Adelphi Hotel has been restored to its original state. The first Roosevelt bathhouse is being refurbished, and plans are under review to convert the second into a European-style spa.

Through the 1950s, Saratoga water was used to treat various ailments, including heart disease, asthma, and rheumatism, but its medical effectiveness has since been discredited in a series of malpractice suits. No claims about the water's curative powers are made any longer, but still people come; they remember history. And the water tastes good.

Calistoga

Legend has it that Sam Brannan, the founder of Calistoga, had intended to name it "Saratoga of California" after the Eastern spa he favored, but he was drunk and slurred his words; what came out was "Calistoga of Sarifornia." It caught on.

Located at the northern end of the Napa Valley, the great wine-producing region of California, Calistoga sits on top of what appears to be an unlimited supply of hot bubbling waters, shooting geysers, and hissing steam vents. It is a mysterious place, capable of creating a great deal of thermonuclear energy. The Pomo and Mayacamas Indians were already benefiting from its waters when the pioneer settlers arrived in Calistoga in 1830. By the turn of the twentieth century, the Indian tribes had long since been edged out of the valley, and the town had established thirty spas. Each had a wooden hotel, gardens, and a bathhouse. Calistoga also boasted its own racetrack. People traveled from San Francisco by ferry or train and covered the final miles by horse or canoe.

It is still a popular spa town, with several establishments, offering various water and mud treatments, but for the most part it is designed to attract short-term guests, because it lacks the more luxurious accommodations of some of its neighbors in the tourist-rich Napa Valley. But a mud bath in Calistoga is worth a try.

LEFT: Mud baths, Calistoga, California.

RIGHT: Interior, Sonoma Mission Inn and Spa, Boyes Hot Springs, California.

Boyes Hot Springs and Sonoma Mission Inn

"The whole neighborhood of Mount Saint Helena is full of sulfur and of boiling springs . . . and Calistoga itself seems to repose on a mere film above a boiling subterranean lake," wrote Robert Louis Stevenson in *The Silverado Squatters.* He was referring to Sonoma Valley, which lies just over a ridge from Calistoga. Here as well, drawn to the healing power of its underground springs, Indians were the first to discover the valley's treasures. They gave it the enchanting name "Valley of the Moon" and considered it a sacred healing ground.

In 1895, workers drilling on the property of a Captain and Mrs. Boyes made a discovery that would soon lead to one of Sonoma Valley's biggest attractions—the Boyes hot springs. The water had a temperature of 112 de-

FACING PAGE: Interior, Sutro Baths, San Francisco, ca. 1900, lithograph.

grees Fahrenheit and contained an immense volume of natural gas, reputedly enough to supply the entire city of Sonoma with light. The Boyes Hot Springs Resort was soon established. When San Francisco's well-to-do learned of the spa, they flocked by boat and stagecoach to this haven for romantics, lovers of pleasure, and seekers of health.

In 1928 the Boyes Hot Springs Resort became the Sonoma Mission Inn and Spa. The new building was a replica of a California mission, complete with an arcade and a bell tower. The bathhouse was very up-to-date and

In 1881 Adolph Sutro bought most of the western headlands of San Francisco. Five years later the Sutro Baths, spread over three acres, opened to a dazzled public. The artistic detail and engineering ingenuity of the bathhouse was impressive. A classic Greek portal opened onto a massive glass enclosure containing one freshwater tank, five saltwater tanks at various temperatures, and a large saltwater tank at ocean temperature. Its three restaurants could seat one thousand people at a time. Its galleries exhibited art from all over the world and its amphitheater, seating 3,700, presented a variety of performances. The Sutro Baths could accommodate 25,000 people a day and it cost ten cents to get in.

When the popularity of public baths waned in the twentieth century, the baths were converted into an ice-skating rink that was destroyed by fire in 1966.

enjoyed the reputation of having the finest and largest mineral-water swimming pool in the world. After World War II the inn was used as a recovery center for wounded veterans. The hot springs underneath are now dormant, but recently the owners received a grant to study the waters.

In 1981 the resort was remodeled as a well-equipped European-style spa with elegant accommodations. It offers body treatments such as massage and aromatherapy, beauty treatments, and fitness classes. Its two restaurants serve the finest California wines and exquisite California cuisine, including an optional low-calorie menu. Surrounded by eight acres of eucalyptus-shaded grounds and just a short drive from San Francisco, the Sonoma Mission Inn and Spa is the quintessential California resort.

Boating at Boyes Hot Springs, Sonoma County, California.

Two Bunch Palms

In the heart of Desert Hot Springs, California, amid a desertscape of cacti and road runners, is a large house, knows as Rock House, that was once Al Capone's country retreat. Beautiful tamarisk trees rustle in the afternoon wind, making a sound that soothes the mind. It now houses the main lounge and bathhouse of the Two Bunch Palms spa.

Beneath the property is a slightly sulfurous thermal spring. Its natural artesian mineral waters had served Native Americans and conquistadors, but they gained widespread recognition a hundred years ago when they were discovered by a U.S. Army survey team. A tall cluster of twin palms, the focal point of the area, was designated "Two Bunch Palms" on the army map.

"From my analysis of the water, I have not found the like of them [*sic*] in any country I have explored," stated Dr. Broue, an eminent Viennese metallurgist, chemist, geologist, and physicist, in the 1850s. "What impressed me is the mineral content of the water. The water is a pronounced curative agency and it could appear to have qualities superior to any water known to me."

In 1945 this oasis added a gambling casino and attracted such celebrities as Alice Faye, Errol Flynn, and Jack Dempsey, who came here to gamble as well as to take the waters and salt rubs. It is still a popular hideout for the entertainment industry.

Much emphasis is put on the water, which bubbles out of the ground at a scalding 165 degrees Fahrenheit and flows freely into a series of pools, then continues through a channel that runs in front of Rock House and out to the desert. The bathhouse has an indoor spa with a great assortment of body pamperings—massage, salt glow, reflexology, facials, and hair treatments. The grottolike pool area is graced by lovely flora and fauna—jasmine, oleander, and tamarisk trees, rabbits and road runners. The solitude is disturbed only by the gurgling of the hot water as it flows into the pools. It is easy to understand why Capone chose this place as a retreat. It truly gives one a feeling of escape.

Thermal pools, Two Bunch Palms, Desert Hot Springs, California.

Super Spas

During the last two decades new spas have been sprouting up all across the country; there are approximately two hundred of them now, serving various needs—from nonsmoking and weight-reducing spas to places where only mothers and daughters go for special weeks. While some spas are viewed as sanctuaries for people recuperating from personal crises and doing inner search, most are places to get a good workout, clean out one's system, and feel pampered. As highly effective stress-reducing centers, spas have once again become favored vacation resorts.

What distinguishes exclusive American spas from the great watering holes of the Old World is their focus on privacy. Several of them—Golden Door, Cal-a-Vie, Canyon Ranch, Rancho La Puerta—are self-contained enclaves completely separated from the world. Although guests can come and go at will, there is not much incentive to do so. These spa centers are designed in such a way that it is possible to enjoy total privacy. Guests are encouraged to select the programs they really want to participate in and to take time for themselves when they need to.

In the cocoonlike atmosphere of spas, the real world ceases to exist for a week or two. Minds are emptied day by day and stress begins to abate. As defensive masks are peeled away, it is easier to relax and be vulnerable.

Modern spas encourage guests to have as little contact with the outside world as possible. Although I have heard of executives bringing their own fax machines and cordless phones, most accommodations are free of telephones and television sets. Any possibility of outside disturbance is eliminated. At Cal-a-Vie in southern California, for example, couples are given separate, nonadjoining rooms so that they can have all the privacy and rest they need and avoid slipping into the habit of taking care of each other. When I went there with my husband, I was slightly nonplussed at first by this arrangement, but after a couple of days I realized how wonderful it felt to read in bed, or take a nap after an exhausting hike, if I felt like it, without worrying about somebody else's needs. Of course there is constant traffic between the rooms at night, and especially for longtime couples, there is something delightfully romantic about asking before sleep, "Your place or mine?"

In the most progressive spas, the mind is just as pampered as the body. Methods to combat stress—balancing the left and right sides of the brain, for example, and biofeedback—are among the services available. Courses are offered in mind healing, life-style changes, t'ai chi (shadow boxing), yoga, meditation, breathing, visualization, and making positive affirmations.

A healthy diet, designed to detoxify the body, often suggests bland and boring food. Golden Door, Cal-a-Vie, and Rancho La Puerta shatter this image by serving delicious low-fat, low-calorie gourmet meals, all designed to work in tandem with exercise to help one maintain a healthy body and, if desired, lose weight. All these spas have magnificent vegetable and herb gardens and orchards where they grow their own organic produce.

The well-rounded, holistic approach of the finest American spas is not unlike that of the ancient centers of Aesculapius. They are on the cutting edge in terms of the programs they offer. For example, I found all European spas relatively deficient in fitness classes—aerobics, strength, and flexibility. Although some, like Evian, offered a few classes in "cardio-funk," they did not match the sophistication of those available in good American spas, and the instructors did not work as hard on training and monitoring the progress of the participants.

Another fundamental difference between European and American establishments is reflected in attitudes toward service. In European spas it is considered good manners for staff members to ignore clients; this behavior gives the impression that they are there just doing their job, without any personal connection. At Cal-a-Vie and Golden Door, in contrast, I found the staff extremely attentive and enjoyed being treated as an individual and not as just another body. However, I met a European baroness at the Golden Door who did not appreciate the "help" getting so chummy with the clients and left after two days.

What Club Med was for the eighties, spas are becoming for the nineties. The larger ones like Rancho La Puerta and Canyon Ranch resemble camps for adults. The guests are not only instructed in diet and fitness but can also enjoy an assortment of workshops, lectures, and performances, including prayer-arrow making, flower arrangement, cooking, belly dancing, slide shows, literary readings, and films. Because there is no gambling or any other form of competitive entertainment, social and spiritual values seem to prevail.

Since everyone works toward the same goals, spa camaraderie develops quickly. In small spas everyone knows everyone else by the end of the week. Friendships and cliques form, and it is not unusual for people to decide to return at the same time the following year so as to be together again. In one of the spas I visited, a wealthy businessman liked everyone in the group so much that he paid for them all to return the following year. This generous gesture cost him around ninety thousand dollars.

Spas often attract eccentrics who demand and usually get what they want. One man wanted an extensive massage each night before retiring; he threw hundred-dollar bills around and got it. Golden Door offers all guests minimassages every night to extract the last bit of tension from their bodies before sleep.

Spas such as Golden Door and Cal-a-Vie encourage their prospective guests not to pack anything except shoes, bathing suits, and personal effects. There is something extremely refreshing about this, especially for the kind of person who agonizes over what clothes to bring to an elegant resort. Soon everyone is wearing the same sweatclothes, no matter what their worldly status, even at dinner. At these spas you will be given all you need; at Golden Door, for instance, guests are provided with freshly starched blue-and-white Japanese *yukatas* to wear to dinner, umbrellas and raincoats for rainy days, and warm hats and mittens for early-morning hikes.

The appeal of the various activities tends to divide along gender lines. I observed that most men gravitated toward athletics, while women preferred massages and other forms of body pampering. Currently, 75 percent of spa goers are women, most between the ages of twenty-five and fifty. But this imbalance is rapidly changing as men, too, discover the joys of taking the waters.

Rancho La Puerta

In 1940 seventeen-year-old Deborah Szekely and her husband, Prof. Edmond Bordeaux Szekely, a Transylvanian philosopher, arrived in Tecate, a desert valley in Baja California, just south of the border. Deborah came from a vegetarian family and the "Professor" was a disciple of the Essene School of Life, a Middle Eastern cult dating back a couple of millenniums. Through eating natural foods and exercising every day the Essenes maintained a very simple, stressless way of life. The Szekelys moved into an adobe hut and established a health farm that they named Rancho La Puerta, or Ranch of the Door—a door into a new reality. The Golden Door spa was so named because it is a more luxurious version of the ranch.

Rising above the property are the mysterious slopes of Mount Cuchuma with their strangely shaped rocks, some of which are the sites of ancient Indian burial grounds. Traditionally every day began, and still does, with an early-morning hike up the mountain, which the Indians consider to be magic, as do some members of the Rancho La Puerta staff. For centuries only the *kwisiyai,* or medicine men, ascended to the very top, returning with spirit and strength renewed.

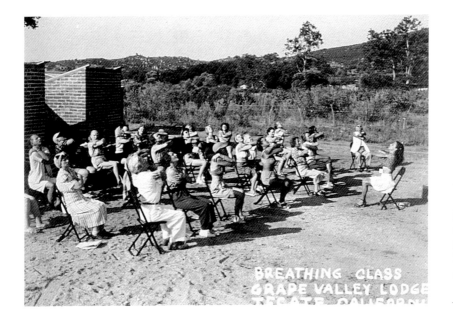

Breathing class, Grape Valley Lodge, Rancho La Puerta, Tecate, Mexico, late 1940s.

When the ranch first opened as a health farm, it did not have running water, electricity, or comfortable accommodations, but it had a natural spring and a stream that made it possible to grow things. The farm offered the first organically grown vegetables on the West Coast, goat's milk, a stream to swim in, and hills for hiking. In the early days the guests paid seventeen dollars and fifty cents a week and had to bring their own tents.

The ranch began to attract people interested in new ways to regain their health in the late forties and early fifties. Soon people from Hollywood began arriving, as did test pilots from an aeronautics firm who had to get into shape to meet the weight and fitness requirements of their job.

Today people do not have to bring their own tents anymore. The ranch is large enough to accommodate one hundred and fifty guests in any given week. They stay in charming colonial-style rooms and villas, some with private gardens, pools, and fireplaces. Each building is decorated with native arts and crafts—festive textiles, bark paintings, and remarkable terracotta objects. The dining room is a fiesta in itself with its brightly colored yarn paintings and weavings. Most of the food comes from the ranch's own gardens; the menu is vegetarian.

When guests arrive, they receive a map of the place and a list of all the activities—at least five each hour—to choose from: aerobics, circuit training, yoga, t'ai chi, jazz dancing, and at times even belly dancing. Although massages, herbal wraps, and beauty treatments are not included in the price, they are available and popular. For twenty dollars I was given one of the best full-hour massages I've ever had from the healing hands of a Mexican woman.

People as diverse as Madonna, Michael Murphy, Bill Murray, Kim Novak, Betty Friedan, William F. Buckley, Jr., and Dr. Jonas Salk are frequent guests at the ranch, an indication of just how broad an appeal it has. It is a choice spa, reasonably priced, with a great deal of variety and a wonderful sense of play. It is an ideal place to bring the whole family, and once people have experienced the ranch, most of them return.

Golden Door

There was a gate leading to the imperial harem of Istanbul called the Gate of Felicity; once you passed through it there was no returning. That's the way I felt upon entering the Golden Door spa through its brightly polished brass door with the tree of life imprinted on it—as if I had been granted access to an inner sanctum.

Located in Escondido, California, Golden Door was established in 1959 by Deborah Szekely, who had been so successful with Rancho La Puerta and had a special gift for creating spas. It became an ultrasybaritic retreat for women who can afford it, except for three weeks a year when it is coed.

It is a Japanese-style sanctuary—the landscape, the architecture, the decor, even the *yukatas* provided for the guests to wear and the lacquered umbrellas for rainy days, all create a feeling of being in an age-old Japanese *honjin,* or hot-springs inn. As in all Japanese gardens, water plays an impor-

tant part in the spa's landscape design. The waterfalls, *koi* (carp) ponds, and meditation pools take maximum advantage of water's visual, sculptural, and spiritual aspects.

Golden Door has forty rooms with tatami floors, shoji windows, and a fresh flower arrangement every day. Each room has its own tiny Japanese garden, where guests can enjoy a private breakfast delivered along with a Zen poem and a fan with a personalized schedule for every hour of that day printed on it. Guests are encouraged to drop all planning and concerns and allow themselves to be fully taken care of. And each day there is a surprise.

Golden Door's inviting public bathhouse has a sauna, a steam room, and a Japanese family tub with jets. It is the place to go to for herbal wraps and nocturnal minimassages. For some people herbal wraps are extremely soothing and nurturing, while for others they are terrifyingly claustrophobic. I personally loved the cozy feeling of being wrapped in layers and layers of very heavy wet sheets scented with a melange of herbs.

The guests are assigned a personal trainer who determines their level of physical activity and helps them through a prescribed program. It is not uncommon to take five or six fitness classes a day. But the ordeal does not seem all that torturous when you know that you will wind up in a serene room where relaxing music is playing and a massage therapist is waiting for you with the massage table laid out—each room comes with one—and the sheets already warmed.

Each day you also receive a facial, a manicure, a pedicure, and a makeup lesson, and you can choose to have a haircut. One needs to be very tenacious to take this amount of pampering. I should also mention some of the fun things you will be introduced to: for instance, I learned to dance the lambada and to make prayer arrows.

Women practicing deep breathing and relaxation techniques at Golden Door, Escondido, California.

It was an incredible joy to wander through the beautiful landscape and pause by a waterfall to clear my mind or lose myself in the intricate dance of the *koi*. "Ask and ye shall receive" seems to be the rule at this spa, where the word *deny* does not exist. Golden Door is a fine rendition of paradise.

Cal-a-Vie

Just as the architecture of the grand European spas imitated diverse styles of vanished empires, so the architecture of new American spas re-creates a va-

Exercise building and pond, Cal-a-Vie, Vista, California.

riety of ethnic styles. Golden Door is Japanese; Rancho la Puerta, Mexican; and Cal-a-Vie, neo-Provençal. For visitors to these spas the ultimate effect of this architectural wizardry is a sense of romantic escape and of getting further away from everyday life than one actually is.

Cal-a-Vie is nestled on a 125-acre tract of desert and wooded valley north of San Diego. During the day the surrounding hills are ablaze with gold and blue lupine. At night you can hear the hooting of owls and the howling of coyotes. The spa was founded by Bill Power, who had been in the business of building hospitals all his life and felt the necessity to create a different kind of place for healing: a place where people come not to recuperate from illness but to maintain their well-being—a place of aesthetic beauty, serenity, and elegance.

Cal-a-Vie's routine is similar to that of Golden Door, although the ambience is very different. The day starts with an early-morning hike into the hills, followed by vigorous morning classes as prescribed on the breakfast fan, and just as vigorous pampering. The guests exercise a lot, drink lots of water and delicious high-potassium drinks (one loses a great deal of potassium during strenuous exercise), and embrace the oblivion of aromatherapy or hydrotherapy. One of everyone's favorite treatment is "body glo," a long-lasting massage and lymph drainage using exquisite essential oils. The spa's hydrotherapy treatment resembles thalassotherapy: guests sit in a deep tub bubbling with reconstituted seawater and algae. The pressure from the jets provides gentle yet effective stimulation of the muscles and the lymph system, improving circulation, releasing toxins, and allowing the trace elements of nutrients in the seawater and algae to penetrate into the body through the pores and replenish the cells.

At the center of Cal-a-Vie is a clear stream that flows through a system of cascades and pools. It makes the most soothing sounds, but these sounds are a masterpiece of artifice. Co-owner Marlene Power, who has an impeccable sense of perfection, felt it was so important to get the sound of flowing water just right that she had an expert brought in from Sea World to tune the waters. By means of hydraulic engineering, the pitch was adjusted until it was not too high, not too low, not too fast, and not too slow; the result is an acoustical triumph and soothing to the senses.

The *cuisine fraîche* of Cal-a-Vie, mostly prepared from food grown in its own gardens, is truly fresh and delicious. Even though the calories are limited to about one thousand per day, you never have a feeling of missing out. Lunch is served beside the cascades, and dinner by candlelight in a dining room that offers the ambience of a fine French restaurant. But there is a special night when everyone eats in the kitchen watching the chef prepare the dinner and sharing her culinary techniques as well as some of the spa's best recipes.

The maximum capacity of Cal-a-Vie is twenty-four people. There were only eighteen the week I was there. On our second day we found ourselves distracted from our blissful isolation in this desert paradise by CNN's coverage of the terror of Desert Storm. Sharing such a powerful experience brought everyone very close to one another. Cal-a-Vie offered solace and comfort at a time when we were filled with deep confusion and grief.

~~~~~~~~~~

I am often asked what my favorite spa is. And whether I prefer European to American spas. But they are like apples and oranges. I am enchanted with European spas because they are filled with history and the spirit of gifted people whose art or music or thoughts I admire. They sustain an air of romance and nostalgia. But I like American spas because the level of pampering is unsurpassed and there is a sense of continuity. All the spas I know have given me different insights and contributed to my well-being in many special ways. I visited most of them at a time of great stress in my life and returned home from each one feeling put back together again. I am convinced that if we are to live the demanding, fast-paced, complex lives we have chosen, it is absolutely necessary to make periodic pilgrimages to spas, just as the Romans did. However, their *thermae* were free for all, whereas the best spas today can put a good amount of stress on one's pocketbook. But hot springs belong to the earth and everyone can enjoy them.

When asked why spa cures work, the prominent French physician Deslois-Paoli replied: "We really don't know. There are two principle reasons. One is the effect of the waters themselves; the other is admittedly the psychosomatic effect. The fact is, the mechanism of many commonly used medical treatments remains unexplained. Why ask more of thermalism?" The real wonder of taking the waters is in the metamorphosis; like the butterfly emerging from the cocoon of the caterpillar, you feel transformed.

Water is a perilous beverage for anyone.
CHARLES MERCER, M.D., from an article in *The Practitioner* (1919)

Taking the Waters Home

Bottling the Waters

"The next four weeks are supposed to work wonders," wrote Goethe to his daughter-in-law in a letter. "For this purpose I hope to be favored with Fachingen water and sage wine, the one to liberate the genius, the other to inspire it."

Seeking the best sources of drinking water dates back to the days before Egypt, Carthage, and Rome. Both the statesman Aristides and the Church Father Epiphanius praised not only the spiritual value of Nile water, but its salutary properties as well. Aristides pointed out that the Egyptians treated Nile water as others treated wine—bottling and storing it for several years. He claimed that they even boasted proudly of the age of their bottled water. Epiphanius was convinced that Nile water actually changed itself into wine. For this reason on Epiphany—or Twelfth Night—the sixth of January, Egyptians collected its water in jugs and, in many instances, bottled and shipped the water abroad. Nile water was distributed as far away as Rome. It was one of the great nostrums of ancient times.

Taking the waters internally played just as significant a role as the external cures. People traveled long distances simply to sample the waters from special springs. "You drink the rain that fell when Moses was in the wilderness," Evian advertises. Ever since 1789, when the marquis de Lessert

Pierrot, the mascot of Spa drinking water, made his debut in 1923. Poster.

improved his kidney condition by drinking Evian water, the town has lured untold numbers of health seekers to its fountains.

In the sixteenth century, clay jars of spa water, carefully packed in straw, were sent to the European capitals. At the same time an Italian water known as Acqua dei Navigatori was shipped by boat to the New World. During the nineteenth century, businessmen discovered a new way of making a profit: bottling the fashionable European waters and exporting them to other parts of the world.

The criteria for selecting bottled waters were slightly different from those for selecting waters for bathing, taste being just as important a factor as medicinal qualities. People wanted to enjoy the taste of the waters they drank; the foul-smelling waters of the sulfurous spas could not serve this purpose. Although guests managed to drink the prescribed amount of Baden-Baden or Montecatini water while visiting the spas, they would not be persuaded to do so at home. Besides, some waters were so rich in minerals that consuming them regularly might pose a health threat. So mild-tasting waters with low mineral content from abundant and effusive sources were favored.

During a vacation in Germany in 1870, George Smith, owner of the *Pall Mall Gazette,* discovered Apollinaris water in the fertile Ahr Valley. A naturally effervescent water with a high mineral content, it was known to relieve catarrhal afflictions of the throat and respiratory organs. Smith im-

The gardens of the Cachat Spring, Evian-les-Bains, France.

ported it to England, enticing the privileged. The Prince of Wales himself favored this mysterious liquid, affectionately calling it "Polly." Because the water business became so profitable for Smith, he soon decided to expand into the American market. By 1902 the White House was serving Apollinaris.

Polly's success inspired other newspaper tycoons to play the water game. In the late nineteenth century, St. John Harmsworth sold his shares in the *Daily Mail* and bought a spring in the South of France operated by a Doctor Perrier. The spring was ancient; there were extant records of its having been a place of rest for Hannibal in 218 B.C. Harmsworth was badly injured in a car accident that left him paralyzed. While delirious, he had hallucinations of bottles shaped like Indian clubs. He subsequently manufactured them and to this day they are Perrier's trademark.

Although mineral water has always been a vital part of people's lives in Europe, the taste for it in America is a fairly recent development. It wasn't until 1908 that bottled water found its way into American homes. Determined to compete with the foreign waters and establish itself as the potion of Presidents, Mountain Valley water from Hot Springs, Arkansas, was the first domestic bottled water on the market. "We have supplied the White House since the days of Calvin Coolidge," its bottlers have boasted. President Eisenhower used it for health reasons and, more recently, President Reagan took it with him to Korea and Japan.

The New Water Trend

In the last few decades, as industrial pollutants have made a large number of drinking-water sources less than savory, and as awareness of health and environmental dangers has grown, so has the bottled-water business. Its product is becoming the fastest-growing beverage in the United States, far surpassing wine in popularity.

In the seventies Perrier perceived the developing health consciousness in the United States and spent over $6 million a year publicizing its water. Within three years it became a veritable cult. Suddenly all bottled-water sales increased nationwide (500 percent in 1990), and other spring waters such as Evian, San Pellegrino, and Calistoga caught on. The popularity of exercise and natural foods combined neatly with concern about water pollution, making mineral water a steady item of the diet.

The *Good Water Guide* quotes the print media of that period. "Welcome to the water generation . . . water snobbery has replaced wine snobbery," wrote *Time* magazine. Others followed suit:

The beverage market has been undergoing a vast mood swing to the light.
Newsweek

FOLLOWING PAGES:
Assorted bottled-water labels.

A revolution is under way. At dinner parties about a third of the guests are turning up with enough Perrier for the entire evening.
The Sunday Times [London]

Americans are seeing a lot of sparkling water at dinner time.

Fortune

Suddenly mineral water has become de rigueur *on almost every dining table.*

The Times [London]

A major shift in drinking habits.

Financial Times

Taking the waters has become a fashionable pastime once again.

The Guardian

The great Perrier conspiracy not only turned a rather modest business into the nation's fastest-growing beverage industry but initiated the water chic. Water has graduated from the generic to the specific. In the eighties clubs like Les Amis de l'Eau (Friends of Water), water bars, and water-tasting parties became fads. Another form of water worship was upon us.

The great rise in social water drinking was a threat to alcoholic beverages. Carefully marketed and packaged imported waters, such as Evian and San Pellegrino, were suddenly competing with the finest wines—and the water brokers with the wine brokers. Several factors contributed to water's stardom: purity, taste, abundance of the source, reputation, and sometimes natural effervescence.

Bottled water began arriving from all over the world—Italy, France, Germany, Belgium, Mexico, even China. The brand names of water became just as significant as those of wine—château-bottled European ones such as Evian, Perrier, Badoit, Contrexéville, Vichy Célestins, Volvic, Vittel, Spa, San Pellegrino, Ferralelle, Fiuggi, Ramlösa, and Apollinaris, and domestic brands ranging from Saratoga in New York to Calistoga in California. Chateldon, which comes from a small source in Auvergne and has gained the reputation of being the most exclusive French mineral water, is referred to as the Dom Perignon of waters. What makes it so special is that it is sparkling and at the same time extremely light. Only four of the best Parisian restaurants serve it: the Ritz, the Plaza Athénée, Maxim's, and the Tour d'Argent. It is expensive.

In 1976 Robert Levin, an American engineer, chemist, and bottled-water distributor, became so enthusiastic that he organized his fellow water fans into a club called Les Amis de l'Eau. The club frequently held water tastings in Chicago and Miami, elevating water tasting to an art.

A glass of Vichy water anywhere in the world instantly soothes the average Frenchman suffering from homesickness.

The pump room at
the Grande Grille
Springs, Vichy,
France.

In 1978 more than four hundred people attended an elaborate tasting at
an Italian-style mansion on Biscayne Bay in Florida, complete with an
eight-piece orchestra, a performing magician, and a wine auctioneer from
Christie's.

Since then, water-related social events have gained wide popularity. In
the fall of 1990, for example, there was a festival in Montecito, a wealthy
suburb of Santa Barbara, sponsored by the American Institute of Wine and
Food and publicized as "Homage to H_2O." Events on the program included
an aquatic feast featuring watercress, water chestnuts, watermelon, and so
on, plus a water bar, a water tasting, and a water show.

Unfortunately, I missed the event, but I have been to several water bars
and water-tasting parties—some "blind." At a recent water-tasting party
some twenty different kinds of mineral waters, their labels concealed, were
poured for the participants. We all had rating cards and judged these waters
on the basis of taste, mineral content, effervescence, and so on. The tasters
were not allowed to smoke or drink wine during the event. Some of the
water experts pointed out that water tasting was highly subjective and required a lot more sensitivity than wine tasting because water, a universal
solvent, tends to take on even the subtlest fragrances in the environment,
such as perfume. Others claimed that it required palate to cultivate a taste
for water. The beginners preferred sweet-tasting and mild waters, just as
novice wine drinkers prefer light rosé wines. More experienced water con-
noisseurs favored greater bite and tang.

Banking on the new water craze, water bars serving nothing but a large assortment of bottled water from all over the world have sprung up in large cities. Fine mineral water from a distant and exotic region might cost as much as twenty dollars a bottle at these bars. To appeal to people concerned about the water consumption of their pets, one bar even offered a bottled mineral water for dogs called Thirsty Pup.

The ambience of water bars is quiet and peaceful, with minimalist decor in muted pastels and whites to soothe the senses. Elegant white leather beanbags have replaced hard chairs. Neither smoking nor wild music is allowed. Some water bars offer tactile delights such as crystals to touch (although one proprietor told me he had to give up crystals because people were stealing them). Large video screens project moving images of dolphins, waves, and clouds. In the background soothing space music, carrying Windham Hill labels, plays softly.

Water bars are not meant to be an alternative to regular bars but a complement to them. After a night of club-hopping and having one's senses overstimulated, going to a water bar has a calming effect and imparts a curious sense of balance. How very California! Not true: New York has water bars, and Paris was boasting them almost a decade ago. Obviously, such bars are not simply glorified vendors of bottled water but a statement of society's priorities.

Water pollution has focused our attention on clean spring waters, and new information about the physical and psychological effects of alcohol consumption has inspired people to "clean out" their systems and turn to water. Awareness that soft drinks contain a great deal of sugar and lack nutrients has also steered the health-conscious toward water. We are back at the beginning: *mens sana in corpore sano.* With the cleansing of the body comes the cleansing of the mind.

More than a thousand water-bottling companies around the world are members of the International Bottled Water Association. As has happened in the beer and soft-drink industries, some of the larger water companies have been buying out smaller ones. Foreign conglomerates such as Perrier, Evian, and Suntory have been making acquisitions at an enormously fast pace. Evian, for example, acquired Saratoga Springs mineral water from Anheuser-Busch and now is a major producer. Perrier has established itself as the largest purveyor of water in the world by buying out other water companies, such as Calistoga in Napa and Arrowhead in Los Angeles. Large domestic corporations such as Clorox and Westinghouse have begun testing the waters as well. The rumor is that Coca-Cola and Pepsi-Cola are planning to enter the market in a big way.

As a result, the market is replete with bottled water of all kinds, appealing to a wide variety of tastes. Not only are there many different brands,

but they often come in different flavors—lemon, orange, lime, and raspberry, for instance—some of them artificial. The reason for this innovative marketing ploy is the assumption that most Americans have been brought up on flavored soft drinks.

Some spring waters, such as Evian and Volvic, are naturally still. Other still waters are labeled spring waters when they are in fact city water that has been processed repeatedly to filter out chlorine and other abrasives. Some waters, such as Badoit and Apollinaris, are naturally effervescent. Others, like San Pellegrino, come out of the earth still and are carbonated later. Perrier advertises itself as naturally sparkling when in fact it has not bubbled up to the surface without processing since at least 1956; it is pumped from the ground through a pipe and then combined with processed gas. A significant portion of Perrier is recent rainwater, and not of ancient origin as the company claims. This false claim created an enormous controversy; New York State sued Perrier over it and won. The Federal Trade Commission and the Food and Drug Administration have asked Perrier to refrain from misrepresentation in labeling and advertising.

Most imported mineral waters are bottled at the source and governed by strict regulations to ensure their purity. Painstaking measures are taken to keep the flavor and carbonation consistent and to guard against polluting substances. In Evian, for example, a barred gate leads to a heavy metal door resembling a bank safe, which protects the tunnel to the source. Still, accidents do occur. In 1990 benzene, a carcinogen, was discovered in Perrier, and every bottle had to be taken off the market worldwide. The benzene was eventually traced to the charcoal filter at Perrier's bottling plant in France. After the recall, its worldwide share of the bottled-water market plummeted from 45 to about 21 percent.

It was an awe-inspiring experience to visit enormous water plants such as the one in Amphion-les-Bains, which produces Evian, the most consumed water in the world, exported to more than a hundred countries. BSN, the company that owns Evian, also produces Badoit, Lyonnais, Athlon (a high-energy drink for athletes), and Saratoga water in the United States. The Evian source is seven miles away from the plant, and the water is brought to the plant through a stainless-steel pipe.

The plant produces four million plastic bottles a day on the premises and is operational twenty-four hours a day, seven days a week. It takes thirty minutes from the time the water comes through the pipe until it is bottled, crated, and loaded onto trains. More than 220 railroad cars leave Evian daily. One wonders how long the source can continue producing at this rate. Will some springs dry up? Will we someday have synthetic water?

Mineral Waters

If we take into consideration theosophist Theodor Schwenk's theory that water naturally moves in an S-shaped way and that by channeling it through straight aqueducts or pipes we are stripping it of its natural qualities, then the only good water is that which comes from a natural spring at its own source, provided the spring is not polluted or overstressed with minerals. Natural spring waters come from deep underground lakes known as aquifers that collect rainwater after it filters through the earth's rocks and soils, picking up solids and minerals along the way.

The Federal Food and Drug Administration, which regulates bottled water as a "food," has declined to define mineral water. The common definition of it is "water naturally or artificially impregnated with natural salts, especially those with healing characteristics." Some of those minerals are chlorides, sulfides, carbonates, silicates, phosphates, and sulfates of calcium, iron, lithium, potassium, and sodium. It may also contain various gases such as carbon dioxide, hydrogen sulfide, nitrogen, and inert gases. It is interesting to note that many of these waters contain lithium, which is used for treating manic-depressive disorders.

The International Bottled Water Association characterizes mineral water as "bottled water that contains not less than five hundred parts per million total dissolved solids." "Naturally carbonated" means that the carbon dioxide content is from the same source as the water itself. "Sparkling" implies that carbon dioxide has been added to the mineral water.

Water is considered "hard" when the mineral content is more than ten grains to the gallon—approximately a hundred parts of dissolved solids per million parts of water. Hard water contains more minerals than soft water and is therefore good for drinking but ineffective for washing, because it will not lather. Soft water, such as rainwater or water that flows in beds containing no soluble substances, contains little or no minerals, making it good for bathing but not as desirable for drinking. Thermal water is water issuing from hot springs heated by natural means in the earth's crust, such as underground volcanic action or the movement of enormous rock formations. The pH factor indicates the level of acid or alkaline in a solution. Perfect water has a pH factor of seven. Below seven is acid; above is alkaline.

Glaciers and Desalinization

Our underground water supply is not inexhaustible; the aquifer levels have been getting lower and lower. Meanwhile a new type of water is finding its way into the market—glacier water. It is advertised as the oldest and purest water and as prepollution water. Since it does not come from underground, it does not have to pass through as many layers of sediment as spring water, collecting solids along the way. "It flows from melting snow flats on the glacial tundra far from the industrialized world and harmful pollutants," the Glaciér Water Company's advertisement reads. As opposed to Evian, which contains 300 parts per million dissolved solids, and Perrier, which contains 505 parts per million dissolved solids, Glaciér contains only 1.5 parts per million dissolved solids. It is beautifully packaged—the disposable sports bottles are created by the world-renowned designer Philippe Starck, who is also responsible for the Royalton and Paramount hotels in New York City. Especially when served chilled, it gives one a cool, delicious feeling.

Most of the earth's fresh water remains frozen in mountain glaciers and the polar icecaps. Glaciers are formed from snow that has piled up for thousands of years, the layers packed lightly one on top of another. Icebergs are pieces of glaciers that break off and float through the oceans toward warmer currents, where they eventually melt. Each year approximately 4.5 cubic miles of glaciers become icebergs—more than enough to satisfy the annual water demand of the entire world population. A cubic mile of water contains over a billion gallons.

Countries with arid climates are exploring the possibilities of towing icebergs into their harbors and melting them down for their water supply. Not only would this be a costly operation, but the presence of a large iceberg would drastically affect weather conditions, upsetting the ecological balance by creating such new elements as heavy clouds of fog.

One water source that has been tapped only lightly is, of course, the ocean. Desalinization plants have been successful in arid areas such as Israel and Saudi Arabia, and they are currently being worked on in the United States as well. If the costs can be brought down, ocean water may be the utilitarian water of the future.

Threatened Waters

The water we drink in the cities passes through several rounds of filtration and chemical purification. There is no distinction between water for general use and drinking water. In the process of accommodating our domestic needs, we have lost something more fundamental than sanitary values. We no longer see, hear, or taste water. In the words of the French author Antoine de Saint-Exupéry, "We taste it but we never really know it." What we have is dead water, a mere commodity, that will never assuage the thirst of people who love the taste of water. Most animals instinctively will not drink polluted water, whereas human beings no longer perceive the difference between good and bad water. W. C. Fields went on record as a man who never drank water. When asked why not, he replied, "I don't drink water because fish ——— in water."

The endless hydrologic cycle begins with evaporation from the sea, which comprises about 97 percent of the world's water supply. Heat from the sun turns this water into vapor, which rises into the atmosphere, forming clouds. When the clouds condense, water returns to earth as rain or snow, replenishing our freshwater supply. The precipitation soaks into the ground or runs into lakes and rivers that take it back to the ocean, where the entire cycle begins again.

Of our freshwater supply, the remaining 3 percent of the water on earth, one-third comes from lakes and rivers or from groundwater, which is naturally purified as it percolates down through many layers of sediment into aquifers. We drill wells to get to this pure drinking water. The remaining two-thirds is contained in glaciers.

Presently, aquifers all over the world are being drained by overconsumption. The Oglala aquifer in the Midwest, for example, which dates back to the Pleistocene Era, threatens to run dry in thirty years at the current rate of consumption. It would take thousands of years to fill such an aquifer again. Subsidence, the sinking of the earth after ground movement, is another problem. The town of Alviso, near the southern end of San

A fish trusts the water and it is in the water that it is cooked.

Haitian proverb

Francisco Bay, for example, has sunk ten feet, and California's Central Valley has subsided as much as a hundred feet in some regions, putting the area below sea level and subjecting it to recurrent flooding.

When groundwater is insufficient, cities such as Los Angeles import water through large aqueducts. This diversion of streams that feed the lakes in the area has upset the entire ecological balance of the life forms that depend on the lakes for sustenance. Mono Lake, a million-year-old saline lake, for instance, will soon be too salty to sustain life. Ibsen's play *An Enemy of the People,* which deals with a polluted spa and the politics surrounding it, is a metaphor for a society contaminated or polluted by greed and carelessness.

The Prophecy of Water

Since human beings are almost all water, we need water to replace ourselves; otherwise we die. We can go for a long time without food but not without water, yet most of us take it for granted. We take showers in it, flush our toilets with it, do our dishes and laundry in it. It has become generic—always available to us through a magical pipeline.

But when things become overly available, they lose their virtue. The domestication of water has led to its desecration in the modern environment. "Water as a commodity has become a mere 'cleaning fluid' devoid of symbolism and respect," comments philosopher Ivan Illich. In our everyday life we no longer think of water as special and we treat it accordingly, no longer offering gifts to express our gratitude for giving so much to us. But people once did, and some still do in scattered parts of the world. And water responds.

The Cogui Indians, an isolated tribe in the distant mountains of Colombia, live between two sources of water—the Caribbean and the glaciers of the Andes. To them, the mountain they inhabit is a microcosm of the world, and water is absolutely fundamental to their interpretation of the world—in their language the word for "water" and for "spirit" is the same. They refer to the act of creation as "water thinking," and all their teachings begin with the question "What is water?" Water is life itself. It thinks, it is alive, and it needs to be fed. A stream is a baby; a river is an adult. The Cogui system of offerings mimics the hydrologic cycle.

Secluded in their pre-Columbian existence, the Cogui had no contact with the outside world until recently, when they called out, making their presence known. They breached their isolation because all these years they have been observing civilization by watching the effects it has had on water. They noticed the diminishing harvest of seashells, which are representative of all of nature's organic forms. The gradual retreat of snow and ice indicated to them the diminution of the entire world. They fear that global warming is leading to the dying of the world and that we are on the verge of destroying the planet. They have blamed Western culture for "selling the clouds" and have concluded that our entire civilization is in trouble today. The water has told them.

WATER MOTIFS IN ART

We have moist imaginations. In them, water is the eye of the earth. A bright eye which in clear pools becomes a mirror, letting us see our own reflections, making each of us the center of a world. In deeper pools, it darkens and becomes somber and unfathomable, hinting instead of drowning and death.

LYALL WATSON, *The Water Planet* (1988)

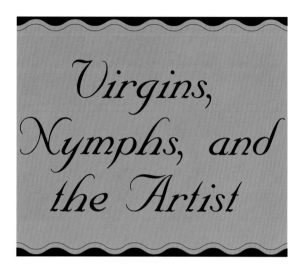

Virgins, Nymphs, and the Artist

Floating Virgins

Since ancient times the cult of water and its related mythologies has inspired artists. Such classical themes as the birth of Venus, Echo and Narcissus, Perseus and Andromeda, Ulysses and the Sirens, and variations on the nymphs have long been favorite subjects. But the fascination with water-related themes reached a peak in the nineteenth century among neoclassical, Orientalist, and Pre-Raphaelite artists, who became preoccupied by the relationship of water to supernatural and mythological characters.

During the Victorian era there was a great revival of interest in such medieval legends as King Arthur and the Knights of the Round Table, and water, representing spiritual power, played a prominent role in the iconography of the legends and similar Romantic literature. The invisible island of Avalon, for example, was accessible only through a water journey. Merlin the magician, like all other druids, had the ability to walk on water and communed with spirits that dwell in darkness and the deep. Excalibur, King Arthur's sword, was a gift that emerged out of water. The Lady of the Lake was alluring and seductive, but she also gave Arthur redemption after his pride nearly destroyed Excalibur.

The renewed enthusiasm for these subjects was sparked by Tennyson's *Idylls of the King* and other poems. Pre-Raphaelites like Dante Gabriel

Pablo Picasso, Les Baigneuses, *1918, oil on canvas, 10⅝ x 8⅝ in. (27 x 22 cm). Picasso Museum, Paris*

Rossetti and John William Waterhouse were especially drawn to the archetype of floating virgins—damsels who had died of unrequited love at a tender age. Such tragic heroines included the Lady of Shalott, Elaine, and Ophelia.

According to the legend of the Lady of Shalott, King Arthur and the Knights of the Round Table were intrigued by a richly ornamented barge with a gold awning that they saw floating down the river without guidance. Inside they discovered the body of a beautiful young woman, the Lady of Shalott. A few months earlier she had fallen in love with Sir Lancelot, whose heart was already taken. Deprived of the object of her passion, the distraught maiden had begun to pine away. One day she wandered out of her father's castle and descended to the riverbank, where she got on a barge and drifted downstream toward Camelot.

> *Under tower and balcony,*
> *By garden-wall and gallery,*
> *A gleaming shape she floated by,*
> *Dead-pale between the houses high,*
> *Silent into Camelot.*
> TENNYSON, "The Lady of Shalott"

In 1861 Henry Peach Robinson produced a photographic reconstruction of the Lady of Shalott. "I made a barge," he wrote, "crimped the model's hair, Pre-Raphaelite fashion, laid her on the boat in the river among the water-lilies, and gave her a background of weeping willows, taken in the rain so that they might look dreary." In 1888 Waterhouse painted her casting off in her boat in what resembled an overgrown backwater of the Thames.

Tennyson's Elaine, the fair maid of Astolat, was another version of the Lady of Shalott. She, too, fell in love with Sir Lancelot, lost her mind, took her life, and down the river she went. Gustave Doré showed her gliding silently down the river toward Camelot in his illustration for the *Idylls*. Photographer Julia Margaret Cameron also produced two versions of Elaine.

To represent sorrowful, pathetic death, the Pre-Raphaelites also embraced Ophelia, whose obsession with Hamlet led her to madness and death from a broken heart. The painter Millais's 1852 version portrayed her floating down a scenic, flower-strewn stream, her flowing tresses bespeaking the end of youth and spring. The model Elizabeth Siddal, Rossetti's model and later his wife, posed for Millais in a bathtub full of water, heated only by a few small candles. When the candles expired, she caught pneumonia and herself almost expired.

Later, ill and feeling rejected by Rossetti, Lizzie expressed her melancholy in the following verse—an ominous foreshadowing of her own death by suicide:

> *I lie among the tall green grass*
> *That bends above my head*
> *And covers up my wasted face*
> *And folds me in bed*

Tenderly and lovingly
  Like grass above the dead.

The river running down
  Between its grassy bed
The voices of a thousand birds
  That came above my head
Shall bring to me a sadder dream
  When this sad dream is dead.

Arthur Hughes's *Ophelia,* painted the same year as Millais's, depicts a pubescent, fairylike girl distractedly dropping petals into a pond. Waterhouse, once again preoccupied with pubescent dementia, painted three versions of Ophelia by a stream. The first (1889) portrays a disconsolate maiden against a fully realized landscape, echoing "The Lady of Shalott." The second (1894) shows Ophelia sitting by a lily pond, absorbed in her private madness. The last version (1910) is a great deal more animated, with the figure of Ophelia almost blindly crazed and aggressive in posture.

The theme of death by water carved a niche for itself in nineteenth-century literature as well. It is often personified by disenchanted women who surrender themselves to the infinitive and impersonal waves as a last gesture of despair. The heroine of Russian writer Nikolai Karamzin's story *Poor Lisa,* for example, throws herself into a pond out of grief for her unrequited love and drowns. In the wake of the story's publication, many young Russian women made pilgrimages to the site and followed her example. Edna Pontellier, the heroine of Kate Chopin's novel *The Awakening* chose her death by walking into the sea, as did author Virginia Woolf in real life. These references might have impressed John Fowles, who re-created the Victorian era in *The French Lieutenant's Woman,* in which his despondent heroine stands at the edge of a desolate quay, contemplating the roiling sea.

Nymphs, Sirens, and Mermaids

In contrast to floating virgins—those poor victims of love who expired on the eve of womanhood—nymphs offered artists a way to represent the seductive and destructive aspects of the feminine. For painters who expressed joie de vivre and pastoral harmony by depicting naked young women at play, water provided an exciting and sensuous playground.

Waterhouse, who frequently painted water-related legends and myths— *The Lady of Shalott, Ophelia, Orpheus and the Nymphs, A Mermaid, The Siren*—returned to this theme yet again in *Hylas and the Nymphs* (1896). Hylas, a Greek prince, was loved by Hercules and became his companion on the Argonauts' expedition. On reaching the River Chius in Mysia, Hylas went ashore to fetch water from the sacred spring of Pegae when the water nymphs, captivated by his beauty, lured him into their vacuous mist.

The nineteenth-century Irish poet Thomas Moore makes an allusion to this incident in one of his songs:

When Hylas was sent with his urn to the fount,
Through fields of light and with heart full of play;
Light rambled the boy over meadow and mount,
And neglected his task for the flowers in the way.

When Hylas did not return, Hercules was enraged and threatened to ravage the land unless his companion was found. To appease him, the inhabitants of the area roamed the mountains on a chosen day every year thereafter, crying out in vain for Hylas.

With the exception of Robert Reid and Henry Scott Tuke, who specialized in homoerotic fantasies involving adolescent boys, most nineteenth-century artists preferred portraying aquatic divinities. Waterhouse achieved a catharsis with *A Mermaid* (1901), in which he was able to put all his aesthetic values and technical gifts to work. The mermaid's loneliness, melancholy, and self-absorption have an exquisite, timeless quality. Her combing of her hair is echoed in the lapping of the waves behind her, creating a sense of eternal synchroneity.

"The wistful-sad look of the mermaid, seated in her rock-bound home, combing the dull-red hair ere she studs it with pearls that lie in the iridescent shell, is potent in suggestion," commented *Art Journal.* "It tells of human longings never to be satisfied. . . . The chill of the sea lies ever in her heart; the endless murmur of waters is a poor substitute for the sound of human voices; never can this beautiful creature, troubled with emotion, experience on the one hand awakened repose, on the other, joys of womanhood."

Unlike Waterhouse's *The Siren,* painted the previous year, in which a young woman gazes regretfully at the drowning sailor whom she has lured to his death, the mermaid poses no menace. She suffers the ontological trauma of being half woman, half fish.

Narcissus

In *Danaides* (1904) Waterhouse portrayed otherworldly and self-absorbed nymphs who, having murdered their husbands on their wedding night, were condemned to pour water forever into a leaky vessel. He chose another classical theme in *Echo and Narcissus.* Echo, a beautiful nymph, distracted Juno so that Zeus could amuse himself with other nymphs. When Juno discovered Echo's deception, she punished her by taking away her ability to speak; Echo could only mimic every sound she heard. One day Echo saw Narcissus by a stream and fell in love with him. He shunned her inarticulate advances, since all she could do was repeat his own words. Heartbroken, Echo faded with grief until her flesh withered away and her bones were transformed into rocks. Nothing remained except her echoing voice, which still responds to those who call her.

Meanwhile Narcissus ignored all the other adoring nymphs and was punished for his self-centeredness. Once, when he stopped to drink at a mountain stream, he saw his own image in the water and assumed it was a beautiful water spirit. Unknowingly, he fell in love with himself. When his reflection did not respond, he pined away and finally died of a broken heart. The nymphs mourned for him, but when they looked for his body to bury him, they found a delicate and sweet-smelling flower instead.

Narcissism became a metaphor for excessive self-absorption and self-love to the exclusion of everything else. Eve suffered her own version in Milton's *Paradise Lost,* book 4:

> *. . . I thither went*
> *With unexperienced thought, and laid me down*
> *On the green bank, to look into the clear*
> *Smooth lake that seemed to me another sky.*
> *As I bent down to look, just opposite*
> *A shape within the watery gleam appeared,*

TOP LEFT: *John William Waterhouse,* Danaides, *1904, oil on canvas, 60¾ x 43¾ in. (154.3 x 111.1 cm). Private collection*

TOP RIGHT: *Jean Auguste Dominique Ingres,* La Source, *1856, oil on canvas, 64¼ x 31½ in. (163 x 80 cm). Musée d'Orsay, Paris*

BOTTOM: *Paul Cézanne,* Les Baigneuses, *ca. 1875–77, oil on canvas, 7½ x 8⅝ in. (19 x 22 cm). Musée d'Orsay, Paris*

Bending to look on me. I started back;
It started back; but pleased I soon returned,
Pleased it returned as soon with answering looks
Of sympathy and love. There I had fixed
Mine eyes till now, and pined with vain desire,
Had not a voice thus warned me: "What thou seest,
What there thou seest, fair creature, is thyself."

Narcissism has also come to represent the challenge of self-confrontation, a journey so deep and unpredictable that the threat of drowning in one's own afflictions is just as great as drowning in the sea:

Beware, my friend, of crystal brook
Or fountain, lest that hideous hook,
   Thy nose, thou chance to see;
Narcissus' fate would then be thine,
And self-detested thou would'st pine,
   As self-enamoured as he.
   WILLIAM COWPER, *On an Ugly Fellow*

The Bathers and the Baths

The theme of bathers has provided artists with a gentle allegory of life at its prime in midsummer, another pretext for painting the female nude

Gustave Courbet,
Les Baigneuses,
1853, oil on canvas,
89¾ x 76 in. (2.27 x
1.93 m). Musée
Fabre, Montpellier,
France

in a natural environment. Courbet, Delacroix, Renoir, Cézanne, Matisse, Gauguin, Léger, and Picasso all took liberties with their bathers, each in his own style. Courbet's *Les Baigneuses* (1853) shows two plump peasant women in gestures of advance and refrain, clearly suggesting an erotic liaison. The realism of these sturdy countrywomen is a far cry from the ethereality of the Pre-Raphaelite nymphs. In his own *Les Baigneuses* (1918), Picasso took it to the other extreme by painting three women in stylish bathing suits at a seaside resort.

The bathers moved indoors with the Orientalist movement, which glorified the exotic hamams of the East and showed the odalisque in a multitude of bathing poses. In Ingres's *Le Bain turc* (1832), a group of naked women are clustered together in an erotic opiate dream. Jean-Léon Gérôme found a more realistic balance between the architecture of the bathhouses and the female form. Having actually traveled to Egypt and Turkey, he was able to capture the reality of the environment, although he romanticized it afterward with Western models draped in the exotic accoutrements of the Orient. The effect is close to photography.

The Dutch painter Lawrence Alma-Tadema's *A Favourite Custom* (1909) depicts fairylike beauties frolicking in the marble pool of a Roman bathhouse. Although the painting imparts a fine touch of sensuality, it has none of the steamy, erotic quality of Ingres's *Le Bain turc*. His women are childlike and ethereal, lacking the carnal demeanor of the women in the Turkish baths. Alma-Tadema used the same setting in *Baths of Caracalla* (1899), reimagining the grand Roman baths occupied by Pre-Raphaelite nymphs and young athletes.

The Source

As spa life burgeoned in the nineteenth century, it developed a sui generis culture, complete with its own gods and rituals, celebrations and temples. Elegant tasting rooms, pleasure gardens, villas, palatial thermal establishments, grand hotels, and casinos were all decorated with the finest materials and craftsmanship—mosaics, frescoes, domes, cupolas, and marble statues. No matter what the form, spa art consistently emphasized perpetual youth and presaged immortality. Allegorical figures from folklore and mythology adorned these secular shrines, with Aphrodite and Artemis representing the polarities in spa iconography—the simultaneous celebration of innocence and eros.

One of the most common icons of spa art is the source or fountain. As a theme it inspired such painters and sculptors as Ingres, Rodin, and Miró. In their art, a fountain or spring was often represented by a nubile young woman, sexually ripe but innocent. In *La Source* (1856) Ingres depicted a nude, pubescent girl in *contrapposto* attitude, standing in a spring. She is pouring water back into the spring from a jug—a symbol of the female vessel and the Great Goddess. Her pouring water back into the source also calls to mind the penance of the Danaides. Nineteenth-century Romantic painters such as Bouguereau frequently associated the image of a broken

Sir Lawrence Alma-Tadema, A Favourite Custom, 1909, oil on wood, 26 x 17¾ in. (660 x 451 cm). Tate Gallery, London

Edgar Degas, Le Tub, 1886, pastel, 23½ x 32¾ in. (60 x 83 cm). Musée d'Orsay, Paris

Timothy Hinchliff,
Cloud Mover, An-
gel of Water, *1987,*
yarn painting, 60 x
48 in. (152.4 x 121.9
cm). Collection Debo-
rah Szekely/Rancho
La Puerta

Some modern-day artists are finding inspiration in the deities and rites of tribal societies, and are reinventing them. "Cloud Mover, Angel of Water, is the ancient rain goddess, our grandmother growth, calls the rain clouds from the Pacific," explains California yarn painter and storyteller Timothy Hinchcliff. "With her sacred goddess staff next to her Heart and a Votive Bowl in her hands she calls aloud. She calls to the deep blue ocean for life to return renewed. With the clouds as her gray blankets she tucks her children in. The People, Plants, and Animals she cares for just the same. She brings the sweet waters that bathe our skin and nurture our bodies. She has taught us to offer all our affection for her rainy days. For we all are the Sons and Daughters of her sacred waters."

jug with a young woman's violated virtue. In *La Source* Ingres gave visual reality to the myths' anthropomorphization of lakes, streams, and springs. With this painting the quintessential water nymph was created.

In 1969 this same image appeared on the poster for the Woodstock music festival. It was surrounded by images depicting spring and love in an attempt to suggest a modern May Day festival or bacchanal. The poster's vision was realized. Youths came together from all over to hear their minstrels sing of love and peace, while they indulged in lovemaking and the consumption of mind-altering substances—synthetic versions of divine mushrooms. The event became the counterculture milestone for the Aquarian Age, the age of the Water Bearer.

Fin-de-siècle artists squeezed the solitary nymph into a small room with hardly anything but a bed and a basin. The basin replaced the source, and the virgin became the whore. With the focus on the body, the faces were lost. Degas's *Le Tub* (1889), Picasso's *The Blue Room* (1901), and Bonnard's *Nu dans le bain* (1937) are all studies in color and light. Bonnard, in fact, became extremely fascinated with painting the bathtub, particularly the buoyant effect of water on the body, and the prosaic act of bathing.

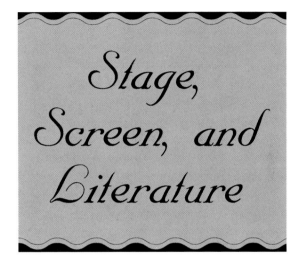

Stage, Screen, and Literature

Water and Cinema

One night I sat around with friends and we played a game of writing down the names of films with water-related themes. Here is our list: *Histoire d'eau, Being There, The Man Who Fell to Earth, Chinatown, On Golden Pond, Greed, Mister Peabody and the Mermaid, Splash, On the Waterfront, Last Year at Marienbad, The Rainmaker, The Last Wave, South Pacific, Lifeboat, The Wizard of Oz, Juliet of the Spirits, 8½, The Rains Came, Raise the Titanic, Agatha, The Wet Parade, Singin' in the Rain, Baby the Rain Must Fall, The Philadelphia Story, Niagara, River of No Return, A Place in the Sun, The Song of Bernadette, Rain, Night of the Hunter, Fitzcarraldo, The Old Man and the Sea, Swimming to Cambodia, Boudu Saved from Drowning, Three Coins in the Fountain, Sunset Boulevard, The Cure, Teenagers from Outer Space, The Poseidon Adventure, Dark Eyes, The River,* and *The Virgin Spring.* There are of course many more. In most of these films water functions as a metaphor. In *The Wizard of Oz,* for example, the Wicked Witch of the West disappears when doused with water, suggesting that evil is rendered powerless when confronted by elemental purity. In Ingmar Bergman's *Virgin Spring* a virgin's rape and death create a spring. *Sunset Boulevard* begins with the narrator narrating from under water—in this case the water is a swimming pool, but the scene has the impact of a dead hero singing from the depths of the sea.

Esther Williams in The Million Dollar Mermaid, *1954.*

Films, mainstream (main-stream) and experimental alike, continue to mine the symbolic strength of water. In experimental filmmaker Stan Brakhage's film *Window, Water, Baby Moving,* water is a metaphor for birthing. In *Fatal Attraction,* the character Glenn Close plays is repeatedly associated with water—from making love in the sink to drowning in the tub and everything else in between—representing the libidinous and fatalistic aspects of water. In *Chinatown,* water becomes a symbol of power and greed: whoever owns the waters wields the power.

The image of the maiden as the source also found its way into the cinema. One of the most stereotypical portrayals appears in Westerns: the beautiful Indian maiden bathing in a stream. When the hero chances upon her, she is startled and covers herself, but this incident often marks the beginning of courtship.

A most graphic example of "the source" is the portrayal of Manon in *Manon des sources,* the second book, and film, of French writer and film director Marcel Pagnol's two-part work *L'Eau des collines.* Manon has a natural affinity for sources of water and personifies a spring nymph with alarmingly paganistic overtones. The first part, *Jean de Florette,* also tackles the symbolism of water. Jean, the good and honest hunchback, arrives in Provence to create a viable farm on seemingly barren soil, but his rascally neighbors are jealous. "He's been lucky to have had a rotten spring, but that's the sign of a blazing summer," says one of them, as he plots to dam

Philippe Halsman, Mike Todd's Peep Show, 1950. Copyright Yvonne Halsman

up Jean's spring. "I'm telling you, by the end of this July all this greenery will be as yellow as ripe corn, and as for the maize, it'll be singing like cicadas."

The most intriguing filmmaker immersed in the semiology of water is, of course, Federico Fellini. From the ending of *La Strada,* when Gelsomina is set against the sea, and of *La Dolce Vita,* with the creature cast up from the sea, to the great whore Saraghina's magnificent dance for the young boys on the beach in $8\frac{1}{2}$, to the scene at the baths of Montecatini in the same film, he constantly probes water's symbolic depths. But the line that lingers most vividly in my mind is from *Juliet of the Spirits,* which was shot in the great casino of the San Pellegrino spa: "When you want truth, Juliet, drink water."

"I came to Casablanca for the waters."
"What waters? We're in the desert."
"I was misinformed."

                    Humphrey Bogart and Claude Rains in the film Casablanca

Jacques-Louis David, Marat mort, 1793, oil on canvas, 65 x 50½ in. (165.1 x 128.3 cm). Musées Royeaux des Beaux-Arts de Belgique, Brussels

The River Journey in Literature

In James Joyce's *Finnegans Wake,* the River Liffey flows through the pages, accompanying readers as they journey through the book. Mark Twain used the Mississippi as the setting for the perilous flight of Huck Finn and the runaway slave Jim. C. S. Forester's novel *The African Queen* presents the survival of the relationship of a mismatched couple against all odds, as symbolized by a voyage through tumultuous river waters and all the dangers they hold—rapids, leeches, and enemies on other boats. In James Dickey's novel *Deliverance,* as a group of men journey down a river, one after the other meets his death.

The Great Bath Murders

A bath is a vulnerable place to be. Not only is one utterly relaxed in the bath but also naked, exposed, and without a shield. Perhaps because of this, baths have often been the sites of famous murders in art and mythology. In Aeschylus's *Agamemnon,* Clytemnestra and her lover Aegisthus murder Agamemnon with an ax while the king and his concubine, Cassandra, are taking a bath after his return from the Trojan War. Of course the murder of Jean-Paul Marat by Charlotte Corday in his *sabotière* has gone down in history, inspiring paintings, plays, and works of literature, such as Jacques-Louis David's painting *Marat mort,* allegedly sketched from the corpse itself, and Peter Weiss's play *The Persecution and Assassination of Jean-Paul Marat as Performed by the Inmates of the Asylum of Charenton under the Direction of the Marquis de Sade.* Well-known mystery writers from Agatha Christie and Dorothy Sayers to Mary Higgins Clark have crammed dead bodies into tubs and set some of their murders in spas. But perhaps the most haunting of water-related murders is the sinister shower stabbing in Alfred Hitchcock's film *Psycho.* Norman Bates, played by Anthony Perkins, has practically become a household word for the rhythmically brutal murder he committed, a murder that has insinuated itself into the psyche of every woman who has ever taken a shower, and that also sent sales of bathroom door locks soaring.

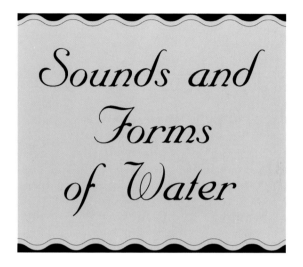

Sounds and Forms of Water

Water Music

Water has a liquid language, ranging from the babbling of a brook to the roar of a sea storm, and composers have repeatedly attempted to capture the moods and variations of water's music. Brahms's *Rain Sonata,* Liszt's *Au bord d'une source,* Debussy's *La Mer,* and Ravel's *Jeux d'eau* are all water-inspired. Handel's *Water Music,* composed for George I, was played as the monarch traveled on the Thames in his royal barge. Chopin's *Raindrop* is a prelude full of melancholy, each drop touching a sad spot in our souls.

Some of Felix Mendelssohn's sparsely dramatic compositions can be considered musical counterparts to the seascapes of his contemporary Joseph Turner. The opening of the *Hebrides Overture, or Fingal's Cave,* is one of the most precise musical expressions of stormy seas, while *Becalmed at Sea* powerfully renders the ominous stillness of the great seas. Similarly, Camille Saint-Saëns's prelude to the oratorio *Le Déluge* begins with lyrical charm in anticipation of a powerful flood, while Vasily Kalinnikov's *The Nymphs* celebrates the erotic sensuality of nature.

The musical interpretation of water continues to flourish. While the Beach Boys' songs celebrate the physical and mirthful aspects of the surfing culture, New Age composers attempt to soothe our minds by integrating into their music such actual water sounds as the pounding of the waves and the murmuring of streams.

Pat Steir, August Waterfall for Berlin, *1991, oil on canvas, 107 x 89 in. (271.1 x 226 cm). Robert Miller Gallery, New York*

Enchanting Fountains

No discussion of water-related art would be complete without celebrating fountains, which are a unique form of fluid sculpture and delight us with both the visual and the musical variations that water is capable of producing.

Proximity to flowing, splashing, and cascading water stimulates well-being, and contact with the hypnotic, soothing sound of water is known to be therapeutic. Architects and landscape designers have therefore re-created natural water forms such as waterfalls, springs, and pools in artificial environments. Especially in areas of the world where water is scarce, artists have taken great pride in transforming the arid landscape into their conception of a water-filled paradise.

At first, fountains were a part of sacred gardens, which usually consisted of little grottoes with a natural spring running through them; their only adornment was an icon like a carved stone, commemorating the deity or spirit of the fountain. Gradually, more elaborate and decorative expressions evolved out of the same sentiment, resulting in magnificent nymphaea with ornate fountains and statuary.

The Persians, the Arabs, and later the Ottomans elevated the garden to an art form, as they transformed parched desert land into paradise. Persian gardens used water in various symbolic and spiritual ways. Central to their magnificent gardens were elaborate fountains and pools, ornately decorated with tiles inlaid with precious metals and stones. The word *paradise* comes to us via Greek from the Persian *pairidaeza,* which means "walled garden."

P. Coste (architect), Cl. Savageot and Huguet Ainé (engravers), Ispahan, Pavilion of Mirrors, ca. 1839–44, engraving, 76¼ x 104⅛ in. (30 x 41 cm). The British Library, Oriental and India Offices Collections

Fountain of the Four Moors in the garden of Villa Lante, Viterbo, Italy.

The fountains of the Alhambra, the gardens of Shalimar, and King Cyrus's garden in Pasargadae—built over twenty-five hundred years ago—have become legendary throughout the world. These were magical places full of wondrous reflections, harmonious sounds, and ethereal mist.

The Moghul invasions transported the Persian style of garden design to India, where it appealed to the sensibility of the Hindus, who already held great reverence for water. The Hindus built temples and palaces on islands in lakes, such as the Golden Temple of the Sikhs in Amritsar and the island palace of Jag Mandir at Udaipur, emphasizing the spiritual importance of water in their worship.

The Alhambra in Granada, a masterpiece of restored Moorish architecture, is a magnificent sight to behold. The courts are ornamented with flower beds and are enclosed by arcades of airy filigree work, supported by slender pillars of white marble. In the center of one of the courts is the fountain that has become famous in song and story, its alabaster basin shedding diamond drops while twelve lions that support it spew crystal streams. The architectonic qualities of water trickling or splashing through foliage contribute to a magical atmosphere.

The Chinese held the philosophical notion that nothing is more beautiful than nature itself. Chinese scholars' gardens, unlike Western classical gardens, which are built in geometric shapes, conformed to the natural shapes of the landscape. Fountains, springs, and greenery were designed to produce a sense of harmony. The builders of these gardens were required to study art and poetry before they could practice landscape architecture.

Japanese Gardens

The Japanese also have great reverence for the natural landscape; this respect is reinforced in both Shinto and Buddhist philosophy. Gardening is not meant to create structural artifice but to utilize natural formations and topography.

Initially, Japanese gardens were inspired by the island nation's coastal landscapes. On the sites of spring-fed ponds or lakes, early Japanese garden designers constructed hills out of rocks, positioning them to suggest inlets and promontories. An example of this kind of garden is the island shrine of Itsukushima, which incorporated the sea into the sacred design of its Jodo sect. Only the initiates serving the shrine's deities were allowed access to the sacred island, which could be reached by covered bridges winding over the water. Kyoto became a center of magnificent gardens because of its abundance of springs and streams.

Waterfalls, an important feature of Japanese gardens, always appeared to be natural rather than man-made. Depending on the topography, they ranged from wide, cascading torrents in mountainous areas to a multitude of narrow falls trickling in columnar streams in the flatlands. The volume and speed of the water, and the placement and size of the rocks, were the most vital considerations in creating waterfalls. The garden designer's task was to harmonize all these elements in order to form a waterfall giving the illusion of having always been part of the landscape.

At the foot of the waterfall there was always a reflecting pond for meditation and the contemplation of nature. Often, stepping-stones placed in a seemingly natural pattern united the pond with the garden. Most ponds were stocked with *koi* (carp); one could spend endless hours meditating and watching the hypnotic dance of these colorful fish, which sometimes live for hundreds of years and are believed to contain the wisdom that comes from such a long life.

Flowforms

To us, flowing water may seem chaotic and arbitrary, but according to Theodor Schwenk, an extraordinary explorer of the mysteries of water, it has a deliberate pattern. Its ephemeral train of vortices, for example, composed

*The "Emerson"
Flowform at Emerson
College, England.*

of alternating spirals from left to right, forms a figure-eight pattern that simultaneously moves from side to side. This metamorphic sequence is remarkably similar to organic forms, such as the sequential pattern of vertebrae along the spinal column.

In *Sensitive Chaos,* Schwenk wrote that flowing water "continually strives to return to its spherical form," whether it is a meandering stream, a curling wave, a droplet of rain, or a swirling whirlpool. He also observed that rhythmical movements are detectable in various manifestations of water, such as the changing of the tides and the crashing of the waves. Schwenk believed that because all life depends on it, regenerative processes are continually at work within water. Otherwise it would not be the life-sustaining element.

In an attempt to understand the language of water's movement, the British sculptor John Wilkes incorporated Schwenk's theories about water's natural movement into his flowforms—sculptures designed to give back to moving water its natural forms by copying its rhythmic and spiral motions. The train of vortices, which water will create naturally and which can be observed in any stream, is enhanced through a pulsating figure-eight movement brought about by the proportions of the flowforms.

In addition to their aesthetic effect, studies confirm that flowforms also have a positive effect on the "health" of water and on the human and natural environment. They seem to energize and vitalize the water, making it taste different and grow better crops. Consequently, they are being used in landscaped health centers, water-treatment plants, agricultural research facilities, atriums, and urban business centers. Studies indicate that they have had positive results, especially with autistic children and the blind. When water and its vessel are in perfect harmony, they produce a great manifestation of art and nature, reminding us of Goethe's saying, "He to whom nature begins to reveal her open secrets will feel an irresistible yearning for her most worthy interpreter: Art."

A Guide to the World's Most Exclusive Spas

An asterisk indicates hotels or resorts that offer spa treatments but are not necessarily connected to mineral springs.

Austria

BADEN BEI WIEN

Surrounded by sprawling vineyards on the eastern slopes of the Vienna Woods, this spa town is famous for its thermal springs.

> Place to stay:
> Grand Hotel Sauerhof
> Weilburgstrasse 11-13
> A-2500 Baden/Wien
> Tel: 43-2252-412-510
> Fax: 43-2252-480-47

BADGASTEIN

A super Alpine spa situated in the foothills of the Hohe Tauern range.

> Place to stay:
> Hoteldorf Gruner Baum
> 5640 Badgastein
> Tel: 43-6434-251-60
> Fax: 43-6434-251-625

Canada

> Harrison Hot Springs Villa Hotel
> P.O. Box 389
> 270 Esplanade
> British Columbia VOM 1KO
> Tel: 604-796-9339
> Fax: 604-796-9374

A favorite hideaway with natural hot sprirgs, nestled in the mountains near the shores of Harrison Lake.

Editorial Note: We are grateful to Jenni Lipa of Spa Trek Travel in New York for her help in verifying the information in this guide.

Czechoslovakia

MARIANSKE LAZNE (MARIENBAD)

A central European spa of Old World renown.

> Place to stay:
> Ruda Hvezda Hotel
> 353 29 Marianske Lazne
> Tel: 42-165-3061/65

KARLOVY VARY (KARLSBAD)

Once a favorite haunt of the elite, now a sober spa.

> Place to stay:
> Bankovni Spojeni
> SBCS Karlovy Vary 2109-341
> Tel: 42-17-25401/07

England

> Champney's at Tring*
> Tring
> Hertfordshire HP23 6HY
> Tel: 44-2-87-31-55

Set in a tranquil 170-acre parkland estate in Hertfordshire, Champney's is a luxurious mansion and a contemporary spa.

> Grayshott Hall & Leisure Center*
> Grayshott, near Hindhead
> Surrey GU26 6JJ
> Tel: 44-428-73-43-31

Health/fitness spa in romantic Old World surroundings.

> Lucknam Park*
> Colerne
> Wiltshire SN14 8AZ
> Tel: 44-225-74-27-77

A luxurious Georgian country house with its own spa, situated six miles from Bath.

Shrubland Hall Health Clinic*
Coddenham, near Ipswich
Suffolk, IP6 9QH
Tel: 44-473-83-04-04

A palatial Georgian manor house with classic English gardens that caters to health and beauty needs.

France

EVIAN-LES-BAINS

An elegant and enchanting spa town on the south shore of Lake Geneva adorned by Belle Epoque–style structures.

Place to stay:
Hôtel Royal
Rive Sud du Lac de Genève
74500 Evian-les-Bains
Tel: 33-50-75-14-00
Fax: 33-50-74-38-00

EUGENIE-LES-BAINS

Near the foothills of the Pyrenees and the Spanish border, this spa town offers the same cures as the ones Empress Eugénie once cherished. It is also the center of chef Michel Guérard's cuisine minceur.

Place to stay:
Les Prés d'Eugénie
40320 Eugénie-les-Bains
Les Landes
Tel: 33-58-51-19-50

LA BAULE

A stylish spa on the Atlantic coast.

Place to stay:
Hôtel Hermitage
Esplanade François André
44504 La Baule
Tel: 33-40-60-20-23
Fax: 33-40-60-89-21

BIARRITZ

In the heart of the Basque country, on the Atlantic, this spa town incorporates the glamour of the old and the new. It boasts the best thalassotherapy center in France.

Place to stay:
Atlanthal
153 Boulevard des Plages
64600 Anglet-Chiberta
Tel: 33-59-52-75-75

DEAUVILLE

Fashionable resort on the Côte Fleurie in Normandy, offering thalassotherapy treatments.

Place to stay:
Hôtel Normandy
38 rue Jean Mermoz
14800 Deauville
Tel: 33-31-88-09-21

Germany

BADEN-BADEN

The most legendary of the European spas, nestled in the Oos Valley of the Black Forest.

Place to stay:
Brenner's Park Hotel
Schillerstrasse 6
D-7570, Baden-Baden
Tel: 49-7221-3530
Fax: 49-7221-353-353

WIESBADEN

A scenic spa town with sumptuous villas in the Rhine Valley.

Place to stay:
Hotel Nassauer Hof
Kaiser-Friedrich-Platz 3-4
D-6200 Wiesbaden
Tel: 49-611-21-13-30
Fax: 49-611-21-13-36-32

BAD REICHENHALL

A quaint spa town near Lake Chiem at the southernmost tip of Bavaria between Salzburg and Kitzbühel.

Place to stay:
Hotel Axelmannstein
Salzburger Strasse 2-6
D-8230 Bad Reichenhall
Tel: 49-8651-4001

Hungary

BUDAPEST

Several of the city's 120 thermal springs feed public baths.

Place to stay:
Gellert Hotel*
Szt Gellert ter 1
Budapest XI
Tel: 36-1-85-22-00

Israel

DEAD SEA

This salt lake on the boundary between Israel and Jordan is renowned for its dense mineral waters and mud. Its surface is some 1,300 feet below sea level.

Place to stay:
Dead Sea Spa Hotel
Sdom 84960
Tel: 972-57-84-221

Italy

MONTECATINI TERME

Italy's most elegant spa town, situated in Tuscany.

Place to stay:
Grand Hotel e La Pace
Viale Della Torretta
51016 Montecatini Terme
Tel: 39-572-75801

ABANO TERME

Located in the Euganean Thermal Basin near Padua and not far from Venice, this spa town is famous for its fango *treatments.*

Place to stay:
Grand Hotel Orologio
Viale delle Terme 66
35031 Abano Terme
Tel: 39-49-66-91-11

MERANO

A hot-springs resort nestled in the foothills of the Tyrolean Alps.

Place to stay:
Hotel Castel Rundeg
Via Scena, 2
39012 Merano
Tel: 39-473-34100
Fax: 39-473-37200

ISCHIA

An island in the Bay of Naples with spectacular vineyards, olive groves, and thermal springs.

Place to stay:
Grand Hotel Punta Molino Terme
Lungomare Cristoforo Colombo
I-80077 Ischia Porto
Tel: 39-81-99-15-44
Fax: 39-81-99-15-62

SATURNIA

Cascading thermal waters originating from an underground sulfur spring.

Place to stay:
Terme di Saturnia Hotel
58050 Saturnia (Grosetto)
Tel: 39-564-601-061
Fax: 39-564-601-266

Japan

BEPPU

A seaport on the island of Kyushu with steaming hot mineral water spouting out of nearly four hundred openings.

Place to stay:
Hakkuu Sanso Hotel
2473-1, Oaza Minami-Tateishi
Beppu 874
Tel: 81-977-23-11-51

NOBORIBETSU ONSEN

A thermal-springs resort located in a narrow valley among wooded mountains on the island of Hokkaido.

Place to stay:
Noboribetsu Grand Hotel
154, Noboribetsu-Onsen
Noboribetsu City 059-05
Tel: 81-1438-42101

ATAMI

One of Japan's favorite hot-springs resorts, near Mount Fuji.

Place to stay:
Horai Ryokan
750-6 Izuyama
Atami City 413
Tel: 81-557-85151

HAKONE

Beautiful hot springs in the Hakone mountains.

Place to stay:
Fujiya Hotel
Miyanoshita Hakone
Tel: 81-460-2-2211
Fax: 81-460-2-2210

Mexico

Rancho La Puerta*
Tecate, Baja California
Tel: 1-800-443-7565

Set in the foothills of Mount Cuchuma, this exceptional spa offers weeklong fitness and health programs.

Scotland

Stobo Castle & Health Spa*
Peebleshire EH45 8NY
Tel: 44-721-6249

A fine spa in a monumental early-nineteenth-century baronial castle of stone and brick on fourteen acres.

Spain

COSTA DEL SOL

A resort near Malaga, offering a Louison Bobet thalassotherapy center.

Place to stay:
Hotel Byblos Andaluz*
Mijas Golf, Apt. 138
Fuengirola, Malaga
Tel: 34-52-473-050
Fax: 34-52-476-783

PONTEVEDRA

One of the most posh Spanish spas.

Place to stay:
Gran Hotel La Toja*
36991 La Toja
Tel: 34-86-73-00-25
Fax: 34-86-73-12-01

Switzerland

BADEN

An ancient spa town on the Limmat River, near Zurich.

Place to stay:
Hotel Verenahof
Kurplace 1
CH-5400 Baden
Tel: 41-56-22-52-51

BAD RAGAZ

Switzerland's leading spa, situated on the Rhine in the St. Gall canton, near Liechtenstein.

Place to stay:
Quellenhof Hotel
CH-7310 Bad Ragaz
Tel: 41-85-90111

ST. MORITZ

Glamorous hot springs and Alpine ski resort in the Engadine Valley.

Place to stay:
Park Hotel Kurhaus
CH-7500 St. Moritz
Tel: 41-82-22111

LENK IM SIMMENTAL

Small spa resort in an idyllic mountain setting at the foot of Wildstrubel near Bern.

Place to stay:
Hotel Kreuz
CH-3775 Lenk Im Simmental
Tel: 41-30-31387

LEUKERBAD

Hot mineral springs high in the Alps.

Place to stay:
Les Sources des Alpes
CH-3954 Leukerbad
Tel: 41-27-62-11-51

United States

Golden Door*
P.O. Box 1567
Escondido, CA 92033
Tel: 619-744-5777
Fax: 619-471-2393

Great pampering in a Japanese-style setting; seven-night minimum.

Cal-a-Vie*
2249 Somerset Road
Vista, CA 92084
Tel: 619-945-2055

Romantic Provençal environment, very small and exclusive, great personal care.

Canyon Ranch*
8600 East Rockcliff Road
Tucson, AZ 85715
Tel: 800-742-9000

Many activities to choose from, including stress-management programs.

Canyon Ranch in the Berkshires*
Bellefontaine, Kemble Street
Lenox, MA 01240
Tel: 800-742-9000

Fine scenery, mind/body/spirit connection.

Doral Saturnia International Spa Resort*
8755 N.W. 36th Street
Miami, FL 33178
Tel: 800-331-7768

An opulent spa with special programs and group activities.

Sonoma Mission Inn and Spa*
18140 Hwy. 12
Boyes Hot Springs, CA 95416
Tel: 800-358-9022

A haven with a mission-style inn in the heart of California's wine country.

The Oaks at Ojai*
122 East Ojai Avenue
Ojai, CA 93023
Tel: 805-646-5573

Efficient spa in the Ojai Valley of the Los Padres Mountains.

The Greenhouse*
P.O. Box 1144
Arlington, TX 76004
Tel: 817-640-4000

A luxurious, women-only spa offering interesting diversions, such as shopping trips to Neiman-Marcus.

Maine Chance*
5830 East Jean Avenue
Phoenix, AZ 85018
Tel: 602-947-6365

Women's retreat founded by Elizabeth Arden.

Safety Harbor Spa & Fitness Center*
105 North Bayshore Drive
Safety Harbor, FL 34695
Tel: 800-237-0155
      813-726-1161

Luxurious spa around natural hot springs.

The Phoenix Fitness Resort*
111 North Post Oak Lane
Houston, TX 77024
Tel: 800-548-4700

A small, cozy, and casual spa for women only.

Greenbrier Hotel
West Main Street
White Sulphur Springs, WV 24986
Tel: 800-624-6070

The most classy establishment in West Virginia's famed spa town.

Arlington Hotel
Central Avenue at Fountain St.
Hot Springs, AR 71902
Tel: 800-643-1502

The most-favored place to stay in this old hot-springs resort.

Two Bunch Palms
67-425 Two Bunch Palms Trail
Desert Hot Springs, CA 92240
Tel: 714-329-8791

A hideout with steaming springs in the middle of the desert.

Doral Telluride Resort & Spa
Atop Country Club Drive
P.O. Box 272
Telluride, CO 81435
Tel: 800-22-DORAL
      303-728-6800
Fax: 303-728-6567

A full-service spa, complete with skiing in winter and all the adventure sports in summer.

West Indies

JAMAICA

The Sans Souci Hotel Club & Spa*
Box 103
Ocho Rios, Jamaica
Tel: 809-974-2353/54

A spa with complete fitness programs and revitalizing body treatments, rising out of the sea cliffs.

Bathhouse at Gellert Hotel, Budapest, Hungary.

Acknowledgments

I am grateful to many people who have given me enormous support in actualizing this book.

To everyone at Abbeville: Robert Abrams for trusting me once again; my two editors, Alan Axelrod, who initiated the process, and Jacqueline Decter, who patiently waded through it with me; Clifford Browder, who discovered all the blind spots; Patricia Fabricant, who designed a work of art; Adrienne Aurichio, Deborah Abramson, Hope Koturo, Robin James, Rozelle Shaw, and Lori Horak for their extraordinary efforts; and Mark Magowan, who graciously sailed it through the international waters. To Rolf Heyne, Hans-Peter Ubleis, and Marike Gauthier for having faith in a dream.

I would also like to thank Carol Tarlow, Kyriaki Albenis, Arthur von Wiesenberger, Pamela Lechtman, Paolo Belloni, Roberta Frateschi, Claire Burkert, Sandra and Bram Dijkstra, Sandra Butler, Alan Ereira, and Timothy Hinchliff. And Barbara Rosenblum for seeds that I was able to bring to fruition.

My deepest thanks also to people who led me to the waters: Mary Homi and Timothy Fox; Karen Preston and the Leading Hotels of the World; the grandes dames of American spas, Marlene Powers of Cal-a-Vie and Deborah Szekely of Golden Door; Florence Radot and Gilles Janin at the Royal Club Evian; Pierre Barrelet and Jorg Schweizer at the Quellenhof; Walter Wenger and the Baden Tourist Office; Bill Blum and Sonoma Mission Inn; Richard Schmitz at Brenner's Park; Ricardo Pucci at Grand Hotel e La Pace; Signor Baccara at Orologio; the Sinn family at Castel Rundeg; Elke Trager at Nassauer Hof; and many, many others.

And, as always, to Robert Croutier, who tasted the sweetest and the foulest waters to keep me company.

Selected Bibliography

Ackerman, Diane. *A Natural History of the Senses.* New York: Random House, 1990.

Auden, W. H. *The Enchafèd Flood or Romantic Iconography of the Sea.* Charlottesville: University Press of Virginia, 1979.

Babbitt, Harold E. *Water Supply Engineering.* New York: McGraw-Hill, 1949.

Bird, Christopher. *The Divining Hand: The Art of Searching for Water, Oil, Minerals, and Other Natural Resources or Anything Lost, Missing, or Badly Needed.* New York: E. P. Dutton, 1979.

Bocca, Geoffrey. *The Great Resorts: An Inside View.* New York: Hawthorn Books, 1971.

Bulfinch, Thomas. *Bulfinch's Mythology.* New York: Crown, 1976.

Calvert, Albert F. *The Alhambra.* London: The Bodley Head, 1952.

Carcopino, Jerome. *Daily Life in Ancient Rome.* New Haven: Yale University Press, 1940.

Coffel, Steve. *But Not a Drop to Drink: The Life-Saving Guide to Good Water.* New York: Ivy Books, 1991.

Cooper, Patricia, and Laurel Cook. *Hot Springs and Spas of California.* San Francisco: 101 Productions, 1978.

Crismer, Leon M. *The Original Spa Waters of Belgium.* Spa: Spa Monopole, 1983.

Denbigh, Kathleen. *A Hundred British Spas: A Pictorial History.* London: Spa Publications, 1981.

Dundes, Alan, ed. *The Flood Myth.* Berkeley: University of California Press, 1988.

Dupavillon, Christian. *O Royal d'Evian.* Evian-les-Bains: S.E.A.T., 1990.

Eberhart, George M. *Monsters, a Guide to Information on Unaccounted for Creatures, Including Bigfoot, Many Water Monsters, and Other Irregular Animals.* New York: Garland Publishing, 1983.

Fiecchi, Gabriella. *Alle Terme.* Milan: Tascabili Sonzogno, 1981.

Fields, Rick, et al. *Chop Wood, Carry Water: A Guide to Finding Spiritual Fulfillment in Everyday Life.* Los Angeles: Jeremy P. Tarcher, 1984.

Fisher, M.F.K. *A Cordiall Water: A Garland of Odd & Old Receipts to Assuage the Ills of Man & Beast.* San Francisco: North Point Press, 1981.

Frazer, Sir James George. *The Golden Bough.* New York: Macmillan, 1922.

Frontinus, Sextus Julius. *The Two Books on the Water Supply of the City of Rome . . . A.D. 97.* Boston: Dana Estes, 1899.

Gadon, Elinor. *The Once & Future Goddess: A Symbol of Our Time.* San Francisco: Harper & Row, 1989.

Giedion, Siegfried. *Mechanization Takes Command: A Contribution to Anonymous History.* New York: Oxford University Press, 1948.

Gimbutas, Marija. *The Language of the Goddess: Unearthing the Hidden Symbols of Western Civilization.* San Francisco: Harper & Row, 1989.

Graves, Robert. *The White Goddess.* New York: Farrar, Straus & Giroux, 1966.

Green, Timothy and Maureen. *The Good Water Guide.* London: Rosendale Press, 1985.

Grenier, Lise. *Villes d'eaux en France.* Paris: Institut Français d'Architecture, 1984.

Harding, M. Esther. *Woman's Mysteries.* San Francisco: Harper & Row, 1971.

Hart, Mickey, and Jay Stevens. *Drumming at the Edge of Magic: A Journey into the Spirit of Percussion.* San Francisco: Harper & Row, 1990.

Hobson, Anthony. *J. W. Waterhouse.* Oxford: Phaidon, Christie's, 1990.

Holden, William S. *Water Treatment and Examination.* Baltimore: Williams and Wilkins, 1970.

Hotta, Anne, and Yoko Ishiguro. *A Guide to Japanese Hot Springs.* Tokyo: Kodansha International, 1986.

Houston, Jean. *The Search for the Beloved: Journeys in Mythology and Sacred Psychology.* Los Angeles: Jeremy Tarcher, 1987.

Johnson, Buffie. *Lady of the Beasts: Ancient Images of the Goddess and Her Sacred Animals.* San Francisco: Harper & Row, 1988.

Jorgensen, Eric P. *The Poisoned Well: New Strategies for Groundwater Protection.* Washington, D.C.: Island Press, 1989.

Kanner, Catherine. *The Book of the Bath.* London: Piatkus Books, 1985.

Kaysing, Bill. *Great Hot Springs of the West.* Santa Barbara, Calif.: Capra Press, 1990.

Keightley, Thomas. *Fairy Mythology.* London: Bell, 1880.

Kestner, Joseph A. *Mythology and Misogyny: The Social Discourse of Nineteenth-Century British Classical Subject Painting.* Madison: University of Wisconsin Press, 1989.

Kira, Alexander. *The Bathroom: Criteria for Design.* New York: Bantam, 1967.

Lermontov, Mikhail. *A Hero of Our Time.* New York: Doubleday Anchor, 1958.

MacKinlay, James M. *Folklore of Scottish Lochs and Springs.* Glasgow: William Hodge, 1893.

Masani, Rustom P. *Folklore of Wells: Being a Study of Water-Worship in East and West.* 1918. Reprint. Norwood, Pa.: Norwood Editions, 1978.

Mitchell, Stephen. *Tao Te Ching: A New English Version.* New York: HarperCollins, 1991.

Montaigne, Michel de. *Travel Journal.* San Francisco: North Point Press, 1983.

Neumann, Erich. *The Great Mother: An Analysis of the Archetype.* Princeton, N.J.: Princeton University Press, 1964.

Paris, Ginette. *Pagan Meditations: The Worlds of Aphrodite, Artemis and Hestia.* Dallas: Spring Publications, 1986.

Pimlott, John A. R. *The Englishman's Holiday: A Social History.* London: Faber and Faber, 1947.

Powledge, Fred. *Water: The Nature, Uses and Future of Our Most Precious and Abused Resource.* New York: Farrar, Straus & Giroux, 1983.

Reisner, Marc. *Cadillac Desert: The American West and Its Disappearing Water.* New York: Viking Penguin, 1987.

Rollins, Scott. *Painting with Water.* Amsterdam: ADM International, 1991.

Rouille, France. *The Source.* Evian-les-Bains: Société des Eaux Minérales d'Evian, 1989.

Rubovszky, Andras. *The Gellert.* Budapest: Art-union/Szechenyi Publishing House, 1988.

Sarnoff, Pam Martin. *The Ultimate Spa Book.* New York: Warner Books, 1989.

Schafer, Edward H. *The Divine Woman: Dragon Ladies and Rain Maidens in T'ang Literature.* San Francisco: North Point Press, 1980.

Schwartz, Steven. *The Book of Waters.* New York: A. & W. Publishers, 1979.

Schwenk, Theodor. *Sensitive Chaos: The Creation of Flowing Forms in Water and Air.* New York: Schocken, 1987.

Schwenk, Theodor, and Wolfram Schwenk. *Water: The Element of Life.* New York: Anthroposophic Press, 1989.

Seelye, John. *Prophetic Waters: The River in Early American Life.* New York: Oxford University Press, 1977.

Séjourné, Laurette. *Burning Water: Thought and Religion in Ancient Mexico.* New York: Grove Press, 1960.

Sidenbladh, Erik. *Water Babies: The Igor Tjarkovsky Method for Delivery in Water.* New York: St. Martin's Press, 1983.

Simmons, Douglas A. *Schweppes: The First Two Hundred Years.* Reston, Va.: Acropolis Books, 1983.

Smith, James R. *Springs and Wells in Greek and Roman Literature.* New York: G. P. Putnam's Sons, 1922.

Starr, Chester G. *The Influence of Sea Power on Ancient History.* New York: Oxford University Press, 1988.

Szekely, Edmond. *Healing Waters.* San Diego: Academy Books, 1976.

Tsypkin, Leonid. *Summer in Baden-Baden: From the Life of Dostoevsky.* London: Quartet, 1887.

Van Itallie, Theodore B., and Leila Hadley. *The Best Spas: Where to Go for Weight Loss, Fitness Programs and Pure Pleasure in the U.S. and Around the World.* New York: Harper & Row, 1988.

Watson, Lyall. *The Water Planet: A Celebration of the Wonder of Water.* New York: Crown, 1988.

Weiss, Harry B., and Howard R. Kemble. *They Took to the Waters: The Forgotten Mineral Spring Resorts of New Jersey and Nearby Pennsylvania and Delaware.* Trenton, N.J.: Past Times Press, 1962.

Wendt, Herbert. *The Romance of Water.* New York: Hill & Wang, 1983.

Wiesenberger, Arthur von. *Oasis: The Complete Guide to Bottled Water Throughout the World.* Santa Barbara, Calif.: Capra Press, 1978.

Wild, Robert A. *Water in the Cultic Worship of Isis and Sarapis.* Leiden, the Netherlands: E. J. Brill, 1981.

Wilson, Colin. *Mysteries.* New York: Putnam, 1980.

Wood-Martin, William G. *Traces of the Elder Faiths of Ireland, a Folklore Sketch: A Handbook of Irish Pre-Christian Traditions.* 2 vols. London: Longmans, Green, 1902.

Wright, Carol. *Guide to Health Spas Around the World.* Chester, Conn.: Globe Pequot Press, 1988.

Wright, Lawrence. *Clean and Decent: The Fascinating History of the Bathroom and the Water Closet.* New York: Viking Press, 1960.

Wylson, Anthony. *Aquatecture: Architecture and Water.* New York: Van Nostrand Reinhold, 1987.

Index

Photography Credits

Every effort has been made to contact the current owners of the work reproduced in this volume. We would appreciate hearing about any changes in ownership or credit lines so that we may update future editions. Please send this information to: Taking the Waters, c/o Abbeville Publishing Group, 488 Madison Avenue, New York, N.Y. 10022. The photographers and the sources of photographic material other than those indicated in the captions are as follows:

Altgelt-Scott Associates: page 209; AP/Wide World Photos: page 33; Art Resource, N.Y.: pages 30, 108, 190 top and bottom, 196 top; Baden-Baden, Germany: page 132 right; Baden-Baden Baths Association: pages 129, 132 left; Baden Tourist Office, Switzerland: pages 2, 146 bottom, 147 top and bottom; Ian Baker: page 54; Paolo Belloni & Marzia Malli: pages 1, 10–11, 74–75, 141, 184–85; Paul Berg: page 87; The Bettmann Archive: page 96 left; Marilyn Blaisdell Publishing: page 159; Courtesy of the Bridgeman Art Library: page 29; Claire Burkert: page 42; Cal-a-Vie: page 168; Courtesy Casino Knokke, Belgium: page 24 bottom; Paul Chesley/Photographers Aspen: page 102 right; Courtesy Christie, Manson and Woods International, Inc.: pages 5, 193 top left; Colorphoto Hans Hinz: page 24 top; Alev Lytle Croutier: page 144 top; Danish Tourist Board: page 26; John Durant: page 197; FOTEK, Bath, U.K.: page 119; Fotostudio Otto: page 39; Roberta Frateschi: page 122 top and bottom; © Robert Frerck/Odyssey, Chicago: pages 19, 82; Golden Door:

page 166; Robin Groth: page 167 bottom; Barbara Hansen: page 51; Hotel Quellenhof, Bad Ragaz, Switzerland: pages 145, 146 top; Icona: pages 43 (/Foto Mairani), 150 (/AFE/Luca Servo), 207 (/Toni Nicolini, TCI); Frédéric Jaulmes: page 194; Thomas L. Kelly: page 103 left; Das Kurhaus, Wiesbaden, Germany: page 133; Library of Congress: page 152; Copyright © 1954 Loews: page 198; © The Metropolitan Museum of Art, N.Y., all rights reserved: pages 56, 102 left; Andreas Müller-Franz: page 149 bottom; Musées de la Ville de Paris: page 95; Grazia Neri/Shooting Star: page 140 top right and bottom; Robert Nugent Photography: page 38; Jerry Ohlinger's, N.Y.: page 149 top; Copyright © 1956 by Paramount Pictures. All rights reserved: page 201; Beth Phillips: page 204; Rancho La Puerta: page 164; © Photo R.M.N. (Réunion des Musées Nationaux), Paris: pages 4, 12, 21 bottom, 60, 186, 193 top right and bottom, 196 bottom; Roger-Viollet: pages 62, 78, 80, 84, 89, 91 left, 93, 96 right, 97, 100, 105, 112, 113 top, middle, and bottom, 114, 117 top and bottom, 124 top and bottom, 126, 172, 177; San Pellegrino Spa, Italy: page 144 bottom; Scala/Art Resource, N.Y.: page 21 top; Sonoma Mission Inn & Spa, California: pages 158 right, 160; Spa-Monopole Corp.: pages 136, 170; Tettucio establishment, Montecatini, Italy: page 144 top left; Turkish Tourism Office: page 65; Two Bunch Palms: page 161; Underwood Photo Archives: page 155; Woodfin Camp & Associates: pages 103 right (Michael Yamashita), 158 left (© Chuck O'Rear), 167 top (© Karen Kasmauski), 215 (Alon Reininger).

8/60 2AᵁU 3/10/97 9 CIRC